1976

To Worth with Love,
Booie

D0385643

ANTIQUE AMERICAN CLOCKS & WATCHES

by Richard Thomson

Line drawings by Gordon Converse, Jr.

GALAHAD BOOKS • NEW YORK CITY

Library of Congress Catalog Card Number: 76-361
ISBN: 0-88365-350-8

Published by arrangement with Van Nostrand Reinhold Company,
New York, N.Y.

Manufactured in the United States of America

TO MR. H. ALAN LLOYD

*Whose writings first led me down
this delightful primrose path.*

Preface

The interest in and the collecting of antique clocks and watches has grown tremendously in the past fifteen years. Both the aesthetic appeal of cases as furniture and jewelry and the exquisite mechanical perfection of the movements serve to attract collectors to this field. But books on antique time pieces have been too often directed to the advanced collector leaving the individual who is just beginning, or who has only a casual interest, in confusion or ignorance.

This book has been written for those who are not yet experienced collectors. It opens with a chapter tracing the beginnings of time-keeping, then follows the fascinating story through England, our ancestor, to the industries which developed in the United States. The author has chosen to emphasize the period before 1850, considering what follows this date to be relatively too modern to be included in a book about "antique" timekeepers.

Many of the statements made in the text are the opinion of the author and of course may be challenged; however a serious attempt has been made to check all references to assure accuracy.

RICHARD THOMSON

March, 1968   Wynnewood, Pa.

5

Contents

1

The Beginnings of Timekeeping

MAN has always been a timekeeper. For in his tissues there are obscure and delicate biological "clocks" which regulate his daily living, awake or asleep. Experiments have shown that a man confined to the depths of a cave, where there is no daylight, no variation in temperature, and none of the usual influences which make a day or night, will go through all the normal time cycles he experiences on the earth's surface, even with a total absence of means to determine artificial time.

There is little doubt that our most primitive ancestor depended on this kind of physical clock. He grew hungry, and went out to find what he could to eat. This, in turn, may have led to a need for more accurate means of dividing time, for naturally there were some periods of the day that were better than others for hunting and fishing. The sun itself was the first clock, and a sharp eye for the angle the sun made in the sky could be amazingly accurate. From this to the first sundial, which was probably a simple measurement of a man's shadow on the ground before him, was a short step.

As man became civilized, the larger measures of time, the seasons and the years, became important to him for the sowing of seeds and the harvesting of crops. By studying the sun and other heavenly bodies he could predict seasonal changes with great accuracy. It is not hard to understand why the skies were the most important means of telling time for primitive people. That the heavenly bodies took on supernatural and holy characteristics was a normal sequence. A large body of religious data, administered by priests, led to the beginnings of our own sciences of mathematics and astronomy.

Western civilization as we know it began in the Euphrates Valley. It was here too that the study of astronomy was taken up in a serious way. Sumerian cuneiform script was adopted by at least 7000 B.C., so it seems reasonable that such studies were already well under way by then. By 5000 B.C. the cuneiform was highly specialized, and we may assume that the mathematical standards had also been well established. It is to this civilization that we owe our counting systems. The Sumerians first used ten as a base, undoubtedly because the counters of childhood are fingers and thumbs. Later they added six as a mystical number and built a system using six and ten.

Our decimal system is an obvious descendant, and our use of multiples of six and ten for the division of a circle is another. The division of the day into four segments of six hours each and the hours into sixty minutes is the result of the Sumerian and later Babylonian astronomical standards. Consider, then, that the system which we use for time measurement, as arbitrary as it certainly is, has an honorable age of at least four thousand years.

This book will not attempt to delve into some of the more technical aspects of astronomical versus artificial timekeeping. It is obvious that the irregularities in the motion of the earth and other heavenly bodies make variation in heavenly timekeeping inevitable. For our daily purposes it is adequate to average out all these peculiarities and arrive at a mean time.

Our friends the Sumerians and the Babylonians had timekeepers, most of them probably of the sundial variety. All of these were variations of the simple stick in the ground which our prehistoric ancestor used. They could not show mean time, of course, since they depended upon the course of the sun and its variations during the year. Other types of shadow clocks existed, and one very early Egyptian instrument had the shape of a prone letter T with the crossbar raised above the stem. When correctly oriented, the shadow of the crossbar moved forward and back on the stem. If this was correctly inscribed, sun time could be kept.

In areas where most of the days were sunny, and where determination of time at night was not important, the sundial sufficed. But as civilization moved northward into Crete, Greece, and Rome, an instrument which always depended on sunshine was not practical. From these areas came a new standard, the water clock. Although Egypt had night clocks which used the sinking of a pierced bowl in a vessel of water in a predetermined time; or the emptying of a vessel through a controlled orifice, the true development of the water clock, or clepsydra, was the work of the Greeks, who carried it to quite impressive lengths. The effect of barometric pressure and air temperature upon the accuracy of such an instrument was overcome to a considerable extent by keeping the water level in the vessel constant and measuring the outflow. This led to the construction of a clock which caught the outflow from the controlling orifice in a tall cylinder containing a float. The float actuated a pointer which moved upon a suitably inscribed scale. Many refinements were added to this type of clepsydra, some of great sophistication, such as, the striking of hours and a device to allow for variations in the solar day as the season progressed.

One of the most famous of the Greek clepsydrae was that made by Ctesibius, about 300 B.C. This instrument, which was evidently of monumental size, was self-adjusting for solar time during the consecutive seasons. It also was self-emptying, and when the measuring receptacle was full, a siphon automatically drew off the water and returned the time pointer to the beginning of the scale.

Rome had water clocks as well as sundials. One recorded use for the former was in limiting the presentations of lawyers in court cases. To this day, the phrase "He had his water cut off" refers to an attorney whose case has been shortened perforce.

Reference is frequently made to a water clock presented to the Emperor Charlemagne by the Shah of Persia in A.D. 807. It was described as having "twelve small doors, which represented the hours; each door opened at the hour it was intended to represent, and out of it came the same number of little balls, which fell one by one, at equal intervals of time, on a bass drum. It might be told by the eye what hour it was by the number of doors that were open, and by ear by the number of balls that fell. When it was twelve o'clock twelve horsemen in miniature issued forth at the same time and shut all of the doors." This was, of course, a spectacular gift between heads of nations. The usual water clock was content simply to tell the time, and did so for all purposes.

A great fault developed with the clepsydra as civilization moved north. In the winter the water froze. The obvious solution was the development of the sand glass which, while less accurate than the water clock, would operate under any and all weather conditions. (This has survived to the present day in the egg timer found in most kitchens.) The common name of hour glass referred to the usual practice of making the glasses of hour duration, to be turned at the end of each period. It was quite common to have four glasses mounted in a single frame, the first to measure fifteen minutes, the second a half hour, the third three quarters of an hour, and the last a complete hour. In this manner it was possible to keep rather close time, and even to estimate minutes quite accurately. As with the usual hour glass, the entire contraption was turned at the end of each hour. There was a considerable industry developed, particularly in France, for the making of sand glasses. Some literature exists on the manner of preparation of the sand, which, of course, had to be of singular uniformity in order to run freely and equally from one flask to the other. Evidently a very finely crushed and cleaned eggshell "sand" was used for the most accurate work.

There was another time standard used to a somewhat limited

extent from primitive times to the relatively near past. Depending on the material burned, fire could be used for this purpose. The most obvious choice was the candle, which, if suitably marked and burned in a draft-free space, burned down at a constant rate and showed time in the process. Wick lamps were made with graduated reservoirs for the oil. The Chinese and Japanese used lengths of prepared line or string, knotted at intervals. When lighted these would smoulder from knot to knot in a predetermined time-lapse. A similar and more attractive oriental method used a metal receptacle with a groove full of powdered incense. Lighted at one end, the incense would burn down, passing time markings as it went. All of these methods were crude means of timekeeping compared to the clepsydra, sundial, and sand glass.

During the Middle Ages the science of timekeeping passed, as did most intellectual endeavors, into the hands of the Church. It was a practical matter, for it was absolutely necessary for the monastic orders to be aware of the times of the Canonical Hours, and clepsydrae were kept for this purpose. It is evident from examination of the literature of the period that such clocks had means to sound the Hours, either by hydraulic whistles or, later, by the coupling of a bell to the water-clock mechanism. It seems pretty obvious that this coupling was a forerunner of the true mechanical clock, and that it led to the development of a mechanical escapement, as differentiated from the escape of water or sand as a time standard. When this great invention was made, or by whom, is a matter of conjecture. That it was the discovery of the Church is most probable, and that it was developed between A.D. 1270 and 1300 has been fairly well established.

What, then, was this most important invention? The discovery and application of the verge escapement made possible the construction of clocks driven by weights, wherein the falling weight transmitted power through gears and pinions to the dial and hands. While the development of the clepsydra had been carried to impressive heights—indeed, the water clock had been the standard timepiece for centuries—this one new stroke made "modern" timekeeping possible and made all of the earlier methods obsolete.

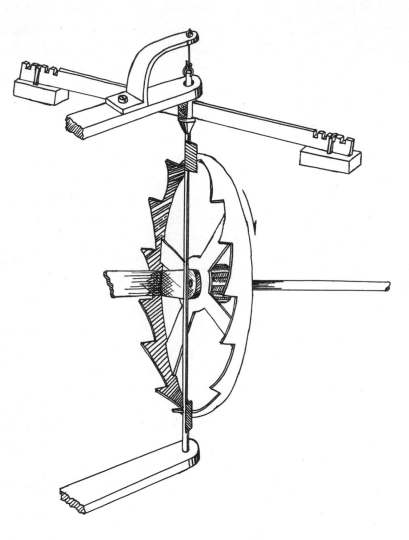

Fig. 1 Bar-type or foliot regulator

The new method used a vertically aligned toothed wheel which engaged a closely placed vertical staff with two projections or pallets. These pallets were placed on the staff opposite the teeth of the escape wheel, which were arranged at right angles to the wheel itself. The pallets were at a right angle to each other and alternately engaged or checked the progress of the escape wheel, which was impelled by the force of the weight falling. The staff held at its top a cross bar of considerable mass, which swung back and forth as the staff checked and was impelled by the escape wheel. The first clocks of this type contained a drum upon which the weight cord was wound. This drum was, in essence, the axle or "arbor" of the great wheel which drove the escape wheel itself. Such clocks had a very short period of running time, but this was unimportant for monastic purposes, since they could be rewound at the time of each of the Canonical Hours. These earliest church clocks contained an alarm mechanism which could be set for the necessary intervals and, in some cases, certainly were used to awaken a tower warden at night so that he might sound the hours on the tower bell by hand. Later direct striking mechanisms became common, first for the Canonical Hours themselves, then later for "equal" hours.

The development of mechanical clocks after this supposed invention date was extraordinarily rapid. By 1320 the method was in constant use, and by 1350 one of the great geniuses of all time, the Italian Giovanni de Dondi, had begun his incredibly advanced planetarium clock. The magnitude of his achievement can be dimly realized when we recall that the astronomical indications of his clock were calculated for a system in which the earth was at the center of the universe, with all of the heavenly bodies revolving around it. This gives all sorts of eccentric motions to the planets, which de Dondi solved with extremely complex gearing, in some cases using elliptical wheels. The mechanism showed the motions of the sun, moon, and the five planets, as well as giving the equal hours, the fixed feasts of the church, the movable feasts, including Easter, and the Nodes, upon which depends the forecasting of solar and lunar eclipses. (De Dondi's clock, which was described in exquisite detail by its maker, has recently been reconstructed under the leadership of the English horologist H. Alan Lloyd and the actual work done by the London firm of Thwaites and Reed. It presently is in the possession of the Smithsonian Institution in Washington, D.C.)

That such sophistication was in existence in the middle fourteenth century is almost unbelievable. De Dondi was admittedly centuries ahead of his time, but even so the science of timekeeping was proceeding at a considerable pace. Large tower clocks made their appearance in most of the capitals of Europe; most of these contained astronomical indications of a simpler sort and, not infrequently, automatons which struck the bells or performed other spectacular activities. At first there were probably no dials, and the time was told by sound alone, for the average townsman was illiterate and would not have been able to read a dial if such were offered. Later, dials of tower clocks were of considerable complexity, and one suspects rivalry between municipalities to produce the most elaborate dial. By 1400 town or city clocks were not at all unusual; in fact, they were common.

The regulator used in these clocks was usually of the bar type, known as a foliot. There was provision made for adjustment by altering the position of weights hung upon the outer parts of the bar. Moving the weights out would slow the swing of the system and make the clock run slower; bringing them in toward the center would speed it up. According to our standards of timekeeping the results were erratic, to say the least. Such a clock might keep time within a half-hour a day, if all went well. The average was probably much less satisfactory than this. Lest we scoff too much, remember that except for church Offices, time was not the compulsive thing it has become today. Life was less hurried, and an error of thirty minutes was probably not emergent.

Along with the development of the large tower clocks, small chamber instruments were being developed, usually as simply scaled-down versions of the large ones. This does not mean that the small clocks were developed from the large. They developed side by side. Examples exist of this sort of chamber clock, now usually referred to as gothic clocks. They were made in Italy, Switzerland, and Germany, and their manufacture continued through most of the sixteenth century.

All of the mechanical timekeepers we have discussed up to this point were driven by weights. A weight was a good motor, for the driving power remained constant during the running period. A clock operated by weight power had one major drawback, however, for it could not be readily moved. Nor could it conveniently be placed anywhere but in an elevated position, where it had space for the weights to fall. This led, somewhere in the period around 1500, to the introduction of the coiled spring as a motive force.

Who was responsible for this most important development is not absolutely known, although the honor is usually given to a Nuremberg locksmith named Peter Henlein. Henlein certainly was responsible for the making of small portable spring-driven clocks which could be worn on the person. These were not watches as we think of them, for they were quite a bit larger in size. (Following this development, watches gradually came into being, although they were not common until a much later date.)

The introduction of the spring drive posed new problems in timekeeping. Whereas a weight-driven clock will retain the same motive force during the period it is wound, a spring progressively grows weaker as it uncoils. This problem, which unsolved would cause a watch or clock with the verge controller to run fast after being wound and slow when run down, was the one faced by early spring-clock makers. There were two basic solutions, both arrived at rather soon after the introduction of the spring. The first, used by Continental watchmakers, interposed a cam known as a "stackfreed" in the train. A spring-loaded shoe bore upon the cam. The cam form was such that friction between it and the shoe retarded the spring drive when wound up and assisted it when run down. This method was only roughly successful, although it had a life of about a century. It was ultimately succeeded by a much better solution, the fusee.

It is not clear who invented the fusee, which, like the verge escapement, was one of the most important developments in the entire history of timekeeping. It was also one of the most delightful solutions of a mechanical problem imaginable and at one stroke did away with the variable torque problem of spring drive. The fusee consisted of a cone-shaped pulley placed between the barrel containing the

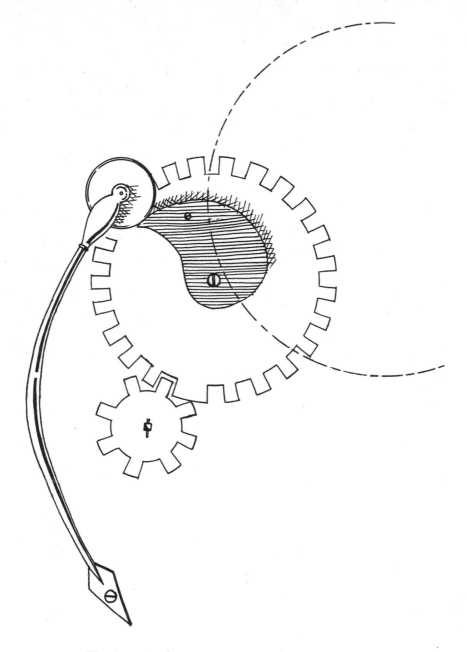

Fig. 2 Spring-driven movement with stackfreed cam

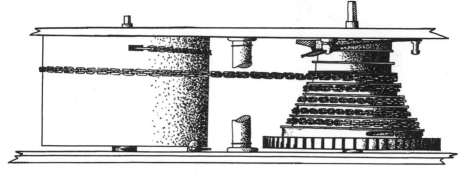

Fig. 3 The fusee

spring and the train of wheels of the watch or clock. A cord or small chain was fastened to the barrel and wound around its periphery. The free end was secured to the wide diameter of the fusee. The winding was done on the fusee. As the fusee was wound, the cord was drawn from the spring barrel, rotating it and winding up the spring as it did so. As the cord wound up on the fusee, it progressively occupied the smaller grooves of the cone. When fully wound, the fusee had drawn all of the cord from the barrel, and the spring was fully wound. The fusee arbor held the great wheel which drove the train. At first, as the spring barrel drew the cord back upon itself while the spring unwound, it was pulling from the narrow end of the fusee cone, at minimum mechanical advantage. As the spring unwound and lost force, it progressively increased its advantage by pulling from larger diameters of the fusee. Finally, when almost spent, it pulled from the largest part of the spiral. It could be easily demonstrated that a correct proportion between spring and fusee would result in almost absolutely constant force upon the wheels of the train. This, at one step, made the spring a competitor for the weight as a motor for timekeeping. The limitations now lay completely in the imperfections of the verge escapement itself, both in weight and spring clocks or watches.

Clock and watch making moved gradually from the original centers in Italy and Germany to France and the Low Countries, although any examples dating from the sixteenth century are exceedingly rare. Watches were being made, although it appears that they

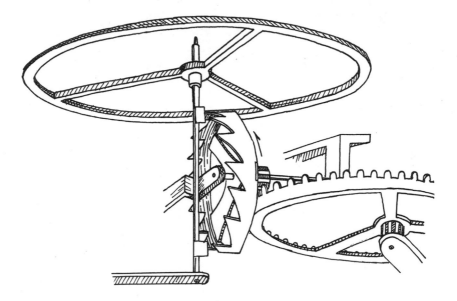

Fig. 4 Movement with wheel of fixed mass

were regarded more as expensive pieces of jewelry than as indicators of the time of day. The first were made of iron and steel exclusively, but as the century progressed, brass became more generally used for plates and wheels. Watches were can-shaped, square, octagonal, oval, and almost any other shape between. Watches and clocks in the form of crucifixes, or other religious objects, were made. In short, decoration was more important than efficiency.

When the portable timepiece developed, the original regulator, the foliot, with its adjustable weights, was no longer practical. In its place, a wheel with fixed mass was used, and the regulation made by restricting the arc through which the balance might swing. In stackfreed watches this consisted of a resilient stop which might be brought into the normal arc of the balance. This, usually a hog's bristle on a movable arm, would stop the balance in its swing and return it before the swing was completed. This would, of course, quicken the motion and speed up the mechanism. Again, such a crude method of regulation played hob with what accuracy did exist in the early watch.

A much more satisfactory method of regulation was used in fusee watches, consisting of a means of tightening the total spring tension. It was effected by a worm gear engaging the arbor upon which the spring was wound. If this were advanced, the tension would be increased throughout the entire wound period, and the watch would run faster. It is true that this would upset the theoretical efficiency of the fusee itself, but it was a small error compared with the inefficiency of the verge escapement.

At this time, about 1600, time measurement had reached a plateau of accuracy and efficiency which was very nearly the ultimate, considering the limitations of the mechanical methods used. The time standards all depended upon the mass distribution of the foliot or balance wheel and, as such, were at the mercy of both variations in the motive power and inaccuracy in the cutting of the wheels and pinions of the train. The degree of accuracy attained seems rather primitive to us, for a watch might be out an hour a day, and a clock which regularly kept within an error of five minutes in twelve hours was a marvel. It was not until the introduction of the pendulum in clocks and the balance spring in watches a half-century later that exact timekeeping became possible.

2

Our English Heritage

T HE science of timekeeping, for science it was in the early days, did not really become native in England until shortly before the beginning of the seventeenth century. It is true that monumental clocks of the tower variety were built and installed in England for ecclesiastic purposes very early, as they were elsewhere in Europe, but these instruments were probably built by continental Europeans imported by the Church authorities for the purpose. Both Salisbury and Wells cathedrals had striking clocks very early, and that of Salisbury, installed in 1386, still exists. The original foliot escapement was altered to pendulum sometime during the seventeenth century, but the remainder of the clock is complete, having been used until 1884.

The European house clock during the early times was to all intents and purposes a scaled-down tower clock. The type flourished in France and Germany, and while precious few examples exist from prior to 1550, they all follow the same general design. That the earliest English clocks should be of this type is understandable, and the development led to the standard English lantern clock which was made in considerable numbers from about 1600 until as late as the beginning of the nineteenth century. The mechanism was mounted in a rectangular brass case, the bell sprung from the top finials on brass arms. The movement itself was in two sections, the time train in front, the striking behind. The wheels and pinions were pivoted between brass strips which were secured by wedges to the solid square plates at top and bottom. The oldest of these were governed by the usual early balance wheel of fixed mass distribution, and regulation had to be made by adding to or subtracting from the driving weight. Since these were domestic or "chamber" clocks, most of them had alarm mechanism as well as a striking train. Some of the smaller ones, in fact, had alarm alone and no strike at all, indicating surely their domestic or even bedroom utility. The first ones had to be rewound every twelve hours. This was accomplished by pulling down a rope which passed over a narrow pulley with spikes in the groove. The pulley was linked to the train of wheels by a rachet and click. In these early lanterns—the name derived, by the way, from the supposed resemblance of the case to a hand lantern— there were always separate lines for the two trains and separate weights. Later, after the introduction of the pendulum, one weight was coupled to both trains, and an endless loop of rope was used.

Generally speaking, the older lanterns were made with quite narrow hour or "chapter" rings and almost never with any other than an hour hand. Quarter-hour markings were engraved on the inside of the ring between the hours and were indicated by the hour hand. At this stage of the game, minute markings and minute hands would have been superfluous, as the inherent accuracy of the clock was limited.

Spring-driven English clocks of the pre-pendulum era are very rare. The reason for this lies probably in the fact that while the manufacture of a lantern clock was within the technical ability of many clockmakers, the construction of a table clock containing fusees and other complications was the work of a master, and at this period in England there were few such.

However, by the year 1622 there were enough native clock-and watchmakers resident in London to be concerned about the evident influx of "foreign" workers. To forestall this competition, they formed a guild which was empowered by the Crown to control the production of timekeepers. This organization, still in existence, was composed of the great names in early English work. It regulated the quality of the productions and, more important, the requirements for membership. In order to ply the trade, one had to belong to the guild.

English watchmaking of this time was evidently copied from German and French work. The productions of such workers as the Bulls, Newsam, and Noway, all dating from the end of the sixteenth century, are clearly of Continental inspiration. During the ensuing twenty-five years, and just prior to the establishment of the above-mentioned London Clockmaker's Company, the English watch became the equal of the best Continental work.

These early English watches were of two general types. The first was of the highest artistic quality, made for the aristocracy, often with elaborate enamel or metalwork cases. The movements were often quite thin, and they were altogether works of art. The second type was quite plain, of rounded oval form, and received the nickname of "Puritan" watch. Whether this sort was influenced by the severity of the Cromwellian era is not certain; however, this plainer form showed a tendency toward solid mechanical accomplishment which led to English leadership in the years to follow.

At this juncture we can pause a moment and look back over the centuries of timekeeping which we have surveyed. At first the sundial and water clock, the sand glass and the burning timekeeper; then, in a burst of progress, the mechanical escapement, the invention of the spring, and the fusee to keep it regular. By 1500 the art of case-work had been carried to heights of beauty we can marvel at today, and the movements in the watch were made small and thin, quite incredible examples of early miniaturization. However, the real purpose of timepieces was not improved. Watches and clocks generally kept just as bad time as they had centuries before. There were isolated examples of refinement of existing principles which had local and limited application, but the use of the fixed mass balance or foliot limited the accuracy which might have been attained, even by the most brilliant execution. A completely new approach to the problem of time control was needed, and it was supplied by the introduction of the pendulum in the case of clocks and the balance spring in the case of watches.

There has been considerable discussion during the past two hundred years as to who was responsible for these great steps forward. When we consider all of the evidence available, we must award the palm to the Dutch mathematician and genius, Christian Huygens (1629–1695). One should note that it was he who applied these devices. The fact that a pendulum makes all swings in (nearly) equal time had been known for centuries, but it was Huygens who demonstrated its use in a clock. Also, springs as restoring forces had been used by locksmiths for centuries, but all evidence points to the introduction of the spiral balance spring by Huygens. This man arrived at the principles and use of these additions in a purely theoretical and abstract way, making mathematical proofs of his assumptions before attempting them in practice. Here was one of the first really modern men of science; his demonstrations were superb examples of pure mathematics.

In one swoop Huygens harnessed a basic natural force—that of gravity—to control timekeeping. No longer was timekeeping dependent upon the inertia of a balance or foliot and the varying force applied by the train of wheels. Gravity is a constant at any given spot on the earth's surface, and as long as a pendulum is kept swinging through the same angular arc, all of the swings will be in exactly the same time. Huygens' application of the pendulum was a simple adaptation of the old verge-type escapement. First he extended one arm of the balance to engage a pendulum hung at the back of the clock and removed the rim and other arm. The verge then caused the remaining arm to swing back and forth and, in the process, impel the pendulum. The constant restoring force of gravity kept the swings equal. He soon progressed to a system in which the crown wheel was placed horizontally and the verge across it in the same plane. In this manner the pendulum could be hung directly from the verge or be hung independently and impelled by a wire or crutch. This was the form which continued in use for table or mantel clocks for the next century.

Huygens' investigations led him to the discovery that the swings of a pendulum were not all made in the same time and that they varied slightly as the arc of swing increased or decreased. This circular error is important in timekeeping, for the force applied to the pendulum is bound to vary as the motive power varies, as the inaccuracy of the wheel cutting absorbs power variably, as the oil used to lubricate the mechanism ages, as atmospheric forces act upon the total mechanism, and as almost countless other minute forces act upon the clock. In order for the verge escapement to work well, it was essential that the pendulum have a considerable arc of swing, or at least so Huygens' demonstrations showed. (More recent proposals have showed differently, but this is aside from the point.) His pendulum swung through about thirty degrees, which made circular error a real problem for precision timekeeping. His solutions, first to gear the pendulum swing down, and thereby to increase friction immoderately; or to construct checks or "cheeks" at the top of the pendulum to cause it to swing in a cycloidal arc instead of a circular one, were theoretically sound but quite impractical. For some years after the suggestions, Continental clockmakers continued to use the cycloidal cheeks, but they were soon discarded in England, for they introduced more problems than they solved.

Huygens was also responsible for the introduction of the spiral balance spring for watches and portable timekeepers generally. Just as gravity tends to return the pendulum to a central point with a force which varies with the total displacement of the pendulum from the vertical, so a spiral spring with the center attached to the balance arbor and the end to the plate will tend to return the balance to a central point of equilibrium. The more the balance is rotated away from the central point, the stronger the restoring force of the spring will be. Here too, then, Huygens solved the problems which had beset the old timekeepers with fixed-mass controllers. The problems which were created here, as in the circular error of the pendulum, were considerable also, and took another century and a half to solve. These involved variations in elasticity and length of the balance spring under changes in temperature. While later of great import, they had little significance at first, since the improvement over the older methods was so immense.

England got off to a fast start using the new methods. The London firm of Fromanteel, of Dutch ancestry, dispatched a young member to Holland forthwith to learn the new method of pendulum construction. While the first Dutch clocks were spring driven, the development in England tended to emphasize the use of weights for motive power. They were applied to the usual lantern type, which in its true form was always weight driven. Some English table or "bracket" clocks of this very early period survive, but they are extremely rare. The most important casing development was the beginning of the "tall" case or, as we know it now, the "grandfather" case. That this was a logical development of the wall clock with weights enclosed is obvious.

The immense increase in accuracy which the pendulum made possible led to the introduction and use of the minute hand in all clocks except those of the lantern type. Why these continued to be made with a single hand for a century is beyond knowing; perhaps it was a matter of sheer conservatism. It is interesting to observe, however, that even with minute-hand clocks the old quarter-hour markings on the inner edge of the chapter or hour ring continued to be used for another hundred years. At first they were kept while the new minute recorder was unfamiliar. Later they remained as an anachronism, ultimately to vanish about 1750.

The earliest case styles were architectural, with their complete pediments and columns with elaborate metal capitals about the door. The cases were generally of ebony, olivewood, or walnut. Sizes were rather small at first, most of the tall cases being little over six feet. The dials were square, of brass with an applied silvered chapter ring. The corners outside the ring, or "spandrel" corners, were at first engraved. Later they were filled with cast and chased ornaments that developed through a stylistic series, which is of some value in assessing the age of a particular clock. The dials were also rather small at first, in keeping with the smallish size of the cases. Later they standardized at about ten inches square and grew larger only as the total size of the cases increased during the next century.

Since these tall cases were important pieces of furniture, they tended to follow the contemporary styles, both as to form and material. During the period of the Queen Anne style, the wood was usually walnut, at first inlaid with marquetry designs, and later quite plain. The door surrounds went from the very early straight columns to the barley sugar twist and back to straight again between 1670 and 1710. The height increased from the early six feet to eight or more in this time and the dial size from ten inches square to twelve. The chapter rings at first were narrow, as were the minute numerals within the minute markings themselves. Later they increased in size and were placed outside the minute rings. Spandrel ornaments changed from the early cherub head and wings through more elaborate cherubs to quite complex designs centering a female or, more rarely, exotic male mask. The winding holes became ringed, and the maker's signature rose from the base of the dial plate to the bottom of the chapter ring itself, and later to a cartouche in the center of the dial. Such dial centers were invariably matted with a fine punch, and all brass parts were gilded. In total, the effect of these early dials was one of elegance. Even the early hands, each a design of the maker himself, were stylistic marvels. From the earliest arrow types the hands gradually became more complex, culminating in the elaborate pierced designs of about 1700, after which they tended to become less complicated.

There was an intermittent interest about this time in Chinese lacquer decoration, and the clock case conformed to the style. The results provided a finish which was almost indestructible. However, while rumors persist that some cases were sent out to the Orient for such decoration and later returned to London, the author is convinced that such instances were so rare as to be almost nonexistent, and that many lacquer cases with a less durable finish were produced in England. These are found dating from as early as 1690 and as late as 1760. The peak period of such production seems to have been about 1735. The majority of such cases have deteriorated to such an extent as to be no longer decorative at all, and some have been stripped to their usual pine carcasses. When a good lacquer case is found, it is a rare treasure. The form and dimensions conform to the time period within which they were made.

Mechanical development proceeded apace. The problem of the wide swing of the Huygens pendulum was solved about 1670 with the invention of the recoil escapement, a step forward which put the finishing touch on the Dutchman's introduction. This invention reduced the necessary pendulum arc to a few degrees. It allowed the use of a much longer pendulum, which was standardized to allow a one-second beat. This, of course, led forthwith to the introduction of the seconds hand and dial, and the modern clock dial was accomplished. It also led to the virtual elimination of Huygens' circular error. Since the pendulum swing was relatively small, and since at every swing the train was forced by the pallets of the new escapement to recoil or reverse slightly, power variations in the train were rendered less important.

The honor of being the inventor of the recoil escapement has been hotly contested ever since it was introduced. Credit was originally given to Robert Hooke, one of England's most versatile geniuses, but later investigations have failed to substantiate his claim. At present it seems that it was most certainly introduced by either William Clement of London or Joseph Knibb of Oxford. Both seem responsible for tower clocks of the 1670 period with the new controller, and both proceeded to make clocks of the usual form in this style. The escapement fast became a common possession of all the trade, and within a few years all new tall clocks were provided with recoil escapements. Moreover, just as many older lantern clocks had had their balance escapements converted to Huygens pendulums, older Huygens type clocks were changed to recoil controllers with the new long, or "royal," pendulums. This style has persisted

Fig. 5 Recoil escapement

to the present day with surprisingly little change. It has proved to be capable of timekeeping within seconds in a twenty-four hour period.

Consider, then, the progress which had been made between Huygens' inventions of 1656, that displaced the old foliot and balance, and the new recoil escapement of 1670. In 1655 a clock might keep time within five minutes a day if it were brilliantly constructed.

Twenty years later five seconds a day, year in and year out, was commonplace. These were scientific breakthroughs in the most modern sense and placed England firmly in the driver's seat in the designing and building of timekeepers.

The cases of the table clocks went through a similar development, from the early architectural styles which resembled the hoods of the tall clocks of the same period, to the elaborate "basket"-topped cases of 1700. All of these were made with a carrying handle at the top, for such timekeepers were valuable possessions and were carried from room to room. Mechanically, many were made with alarm attachments, suggesting a bedside use as well.

Throughout the many centuries we have covered up to this point, all striking mechanisms had been of the same type, known as the count-wheel strike. The principle involved use of a notched wheel, with the notches on its periphery spaced apart in increasing increments. An arm attached to the striking train felt the edge of the count wheel and, once released, allowed the clock to strike until it fell into the next notch. Therefore, it was only necessary to space the notches sufficiently far apart to allow the finger or arm to "count" the necessary number of strokes. Thus, the distance between notches to count two was small and between notches to count twelve was large, with all of the others in between in proportion. This system had one serious drawback, for if the count wheel, which itself was rotated by the strike train, got out of synchronization with the hands, it was necessary either to alter the position of the hour hand or "strike" it around until it again agreed with the hands. Provision was usually made in count-wheel clocks to allow this last action to be performed without extreme difficulty, but at best it was a nuisance.

The winds of change and invention which were blowing at this time brought a new striking method into being. In the year 1676 the system known as the rack and snail strike was introduced by a Dr. Barlow. This system used a stepped cam or "snail" upon the hour arbor. The steps represented the twelve hours. As the hour hand revolved, the snail revolved with it, under the dial. Next to it on a stud upon the front plate was a toothed rack, terminating in a

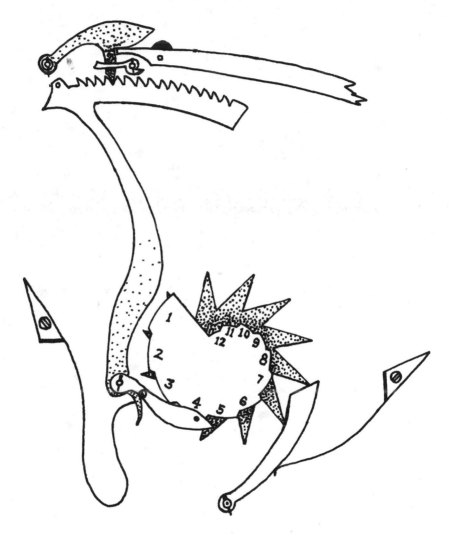

Fig. 6 Rack and snail strike

feeler. When the hour was ready to be struck, the rack fell to the side, and the feeler or rack tail touched the particular step on the snail representing the hour to be struck. Thus, in the case of one o'clock, the tail would arrest the fall of the rack quickly as it encountered the first step of the snail. At twelve o'clock, the fall would be maximum, the tail feeling in to the lowest step. The release of the striking mechanism actuated a toothed pallet which "gathered" in the teeth of the rack, allowing the striking to proceed as it did so. When the number of teeth corresponding to the fall of the rack—and therefore to the hour indicated by the snail—were gathered up, the mechanism locked itself and the striking stopped.

The important advantage offered by this advance was that the number of hours struck was always geared to the position of the hour hand, and no matter how many times the striking mechanism was actuated at a given time, it would always strike correctly. In the older system, actuation of the strike was always progressive, and any such actuation would always result in the striking of the next hour.

The next step forward offered by the rack and snail striker was the possibility of deliberately setting up a system that would "repeat" the time strike at will. Such an arrangement may seem like a useless gimmick to us, but it was a boon in older times when it was most difficult to get a light at night. After it had been developed to provide striking of the quarters as well as the hours, the actuation of such a mechanism—by pulling a string—allowed the time to be heard to the nearest fifteen minutes. Such a striking, with the quarter and the hour struck at each quarter, was known as "grande sonnerie," as opposed to "petite sonnerie," or ordinary striking. Some such clocks struck the grande sonnerie as well as repeating upon demand, and some, obviously designed for bedside use, were repeaters only, with the repeating drive spring wound by the act of pulling the string itself.

Almost all of the table or bracket clocks of the eighteenth century retained the old form of Huygens' escapement rather than going over to the new recoil method. The reason for this was obviously that the new method required a spring suspension for the pendulum, which was rather easily deranged or broken by careless handling of the clock. When clocks were being carried from room to room several times a day, such breakage would be inevitable. It was not until table or bracket clocks became more common late in the century that the recoil escapement was generally used. With several such timekeepers in the house, they did not have to be moved so often.

When the changeover from balance clocks came, it was no longer usual to make the clocks of square section, with the striking train behind the time part. In order for the clocks to be wound from the front, the two trains were placed side by side. It soon became traditional for the striking mechanism to be on the left as we face the dial and the time on the right, although a small number of very early clocks were arranged differently. In the spring table or bracket clocks, fusee drive was invariably used. There are a few mechanical traits which allow a rough estimate of age, but these are not very reliable, as some older systems survived surprisingly long, particularly in country districts. It is not uncommon, for example, to find posted-frame tall-case movements of exact lantern-clock style, with single-hand dials, dating as late as 1780. These were mechanical survivals from a century before, complete with count-wheel strike. Such a tradition died hard in the more backward provincial areas.

The table clock of the period between 1680 and 1760 is a marvel of artistic workmanship, and it is amazing how much effort was put into making all parts beautiful. The pillars which support the plates were turned with central bosses, and decorative fins and grooves were formed upon them in the earlier clocks. In the beginning stages the tradition developed of engraving the back plates with most elaborate designs and of putting the maker's name in a prominent location in the engraving. The backs of the cases were glazed in order that this elaboration could be easily seen. The back plates continued to be decorated in this fashion, although in decreasing numbers, throughout the eighteenth century. The tradition did not completely die out until Victorian times, the Regency examples retaining only a decorated edge and pendulum bob.

The immense progress which English horology made in these earlier years was the product of men whose names have become almost legendary. The Fromanteels, Thomas Tompion, Daniel Quare, the Knibbs, William Clement, John Williamson, and the Easts were among those who made these gains possible. The best known is, without a doubt, Tompion, and his productions which survive are art works commanding Rembrandt prices today.

Tompion was also responsible for a major change in case styling. About 1695 he made a magnificent tall clock for the royal family which had a going period of one year and, among other things, automatically showed sun time as well as mean hours. (This mechanism, which uses a mathematical equation in the calculations that produce sun time, is known as an equation clock.) It also showed other astronomical signs, but since the square dial was not large enough to take all of the indicators the master created a semicircular arch at the top and placed the subsidiary dials within it.

The new fashion for arched dials, which did not become usual until about 1720, persists today. The arch was not always filled with subsidiary indications; oftentimes it simply contained a cartouche with the maker's name. Later it was—and still is—common for the arch to contain a painted disc showing the phases of the moon.

The mechanics of the clock in the period after 1720 were altered only for the purpose of greater accuracy. Tompion's nephew-in-law and partner, George Graham, was responsible for two major clockmaking advances in the years 1720–1730. Realizing that while the recoil escapement averaged out errors by virtue of the recoil itself, he knew that it introduced other significant inaccuracies. He achieved a significant gain in accuracy by shaping the locking faces of the pallets so that when the escape wheel teeth fell upon them and the pendulum completed its swing, the wheel would *not* recoil, but would remain "dead." This "dead beat" escapement has remained the standard of accuracy for all but the most elaborate "regulator" clocks until the present day.

Graham's other contribution to the accuracy of timekeeping was

Fig. 7 Dead beat escapement

an improved pendulum. Most pendulums were made of a length of iron wire, with the weight or bob at the bottom. In situations where constant temperature could be maintained, this was adequate. Where there were considerable variations, as between summer and winter, it was not adequate, for as the temperature rose, the wire expanded, lengthened, and upset the timing of the clock. In hot weather it ran slow, in cold, fast. Graham's solution was simple. In place of the usual metal bob, he used a bottle filled with mercury. The coefficient of expansion of mercury is such that it was possible to have its upward expansion in the container offset the downward expansion of the pendulum rod. This compensation kept the center of oscillation of the pendulum constant under all temperatures. By combining his new compensation pendulum with the dead beat escapement, Graham was able to achieve time standards of greatly increased accuracy, an advance of particular interest to astronomers, whose measurements subsequently reflected this improvement.

Clock cases continued to follow styles in furniture. As the work of Vile, Ince and Mayhew, and the Chippendales became the overriding influences in furniture, clocks appeared in Chippendale styles. Such cases were large usually, even to ten feet in height, and the dials grew accordingly, twelve by sixteen inches being usual, and occasionally going as large as fourteen by twenty. The curved "horn" broken pediment top became almost standard; this is the style which almost everyone identifies as the "antique" clock case. The case trunks became wider and less graceful, and in the productions of the northern counties in England, the trunk became almost as wide as the hood and plinth. The proportions of the tall clock case were best in the earlier times. After 1750 they generally became less graceful and, in some cases, absolutely gross.

Table clocks followed the styles as well, although less intensely. The arch dial became usual about 1720, and the enlargement of the basket top to the "bell" styles came in about the same time. After 1750 the cases themselves began to appear in arched form, matching the arch of the dial. The dials were now often simply engraved silvered plates, although the old applied chapter ring on a gilded brass plate appeared along with them. The interior quarter-hour markings vanished about 1750 and very rarely appeared later. About 1760 a new form of round dial began to appear, and the door conformed with a simple round opening. This was found with the older type of bell top as well as the new arched sort. There were few real variations of these styles, the outstanding one being the balloon clock.

This, an arched case with waisted sides, had considerable vogue from 1770 until Victorian times. The other, more usual sorts reflected the surface decoration variations found in the Hepplewhite and Sheraton periods without varying much from the arched shapes which appeared fifty years before. During the Regency time, a series of clocks with restrained and tasteful brass inlaid decoration was made, and these were perhaps the last of the English table or bracket clocks to achieve real distinction.

Tall cases showed a more studied response to Hepplewhite and Sheraton influences. As in furniture, carved decoration departed with the Chippendale age of mahogany, which had been the primary case wood since about 1745. The general outlines became lighter, and inlay of satinwood, Amboina, thuja, and other exotic tropicals became common. The square dial returned about 1785, and was used rather commonly with the later Hepplewhite-Sheraton cases. The dials themselves had changed from brass and silver to silver alone or, more commonly, to painted form about 1770. Hands deteriorated from the exquisite pierced forms of 1720 to uninspired styles with both hour and minute indicators identical except for length. In the case of spandrel ornaments for the relatively rare, late, brass dials, deterioration was evident, and the form became a series of twisted rococo curves in a poor finish.

The English workmanship was still sound, however. The English clock movement as produced by such later makers as the Ellicotts, Mudge and Dutton, Margetts, the Perigals, the Vulliamys, and a host of other artists has never been surpassed. These movements are as good today as when they were made.

By this time clockmaking had become highly specialized. The maker of a clock acted as a finisher of miscellaneous parts obtained from specialists—spring makers, fusee cutters, men who supplied unfinished wheel castings, hands makers, dial makers, engravers, etc. Only in the very rare cases of a clock which was so complex that standard parts could not be obtained would a clock be "made" in the pure sense of the term.

Several firms grew up in London whose specialty was the furnishing of completed clock movements to "makers" who merely added their names to the dial. Thwaites and Reed, founded in 1744 and still very much in the business today, was a well-documented purveyor of such movements to the trade. In some cases, such as the Ellicotts, the movement would be made by Thwaites and Reed following the sometimes very complex design of the signatory "maker." Records going well back into the eighteenth century describe such efforts for the Ellicotts and other famous "makers." Eardley Norton and his successors Gravell and Tolkein, and Thomas Gammage were others who specialized in this sort of trade. The usual eight-day bracket-clock striking movement was almost standardized at this time, but there were some superficial differences which revealed the manufacturer. This is not meant to suggest that these clocks were ever mass produced. The British always relied upon the most careful hand fitting and finishing, and quality of the results is evident today, a century and a half later.

During this period when England led the world in timekeeping, watchmaking flourished also, and the great makers produced large numbers of watches not only for domestic consumption, but for export to other parts of the civilized world. The application of Huygens' spiral balance spring made good timekeeping possible with a mechanism as small as the watch, and the English greats lost no time in making use of it. Just as good regulation of the pendulum clocks was made possible by raising or lowering the bob, regulation of the watch was achieved by shortening or lengthening the balance spring. This was done with curb pins which could be moved along the length of the spring, causing the spring to vibrate from the point of curbing. At first, the last outside coil of the spring was straightened, and the curb pins worked along the straight section, moved by a worm gear. Later, since the straight section upset the inherent time cycle of the spring, the curb pins were made to follow the curve of the spring itself. This last was the invention of the great Tompion, who brought world renown to English watchmaking.

Watches were always made only with hour hands until the introduction of the balance spring. The vast increase in accuracy which this spring brought made minute indication feasible, and minute hands were adopted. A few other interesting methods of showing hours and minutes were tried but did not last. One of the most attractive was the so-called sun and moon dial. In this case, the hours were told by an effigy of the sun or, at night, of the moon, which traversed a lunette opening in the upper center of the dial. The minute had operated as usual in a complete circle.

Other than the addition of the balance spring, there was little essential difference in the mechanism of the newer watches. The going period was extended to thirty hours or so, and fine chain was used upon the fusee instead of a gut line. The verge escapement was just as before and continued to be the primary escapement for ordinary watches until the early nineteenth century. Movements continued to be very thick compared to modern ones, in order to accommodate the vertically mounted escape wheel.

Cases were still exuberantly decorated and consisted of an inner and an outer case. This "pair case" arrangement kept the inner case, within which the movement was enclosed, dust free. Pair cases are found dating as late as 1840.

Decoration had been a prime consideration in watchmaking before the balance spring was introduced, with its consequent beneficial influence upon timekeeping. With the exception of the plain Puritan styles, decoration in watches took many forms, from exquisite enamel paintings to pierced or repoussé work. This last sort of working and chasing the case surface was in great vogue until quite late in the eighteenth century. The movements themselves were decorated, and the development of the table covering the balance wheel could be in itself the subject for a book. From the simple "S"-shape support of the early German stackfreed watches, it developed into a most complex circular pierced and decorated cover for the entire wheel. The foot or support for this balance "cock" is also of importance as a stylistic guide to date. In the earliest English instruments the cock foot was oval, pierced, and the cock it supported did not quite cover the entire wheel. It was pinned rather than screwed to the plate. By about 1670 the foot had spread out to the plate edge, but still irregularly. By 1700 the foot conformed to the plate edge and retained the elaborate piercing of the earlier watches. By 1730 the foot began to lose its pierced form and was as often as not simply engraved, although the balance cover remained pierced. The piercing itself was indicative. Initially baroque and symmetrical about the center line of the circular cover, it became rococo after the early seventeen hundreds and the rocaille curves were almost random. This general sort of decoration of the cock was universal and persisted quite late into the eighteenth century. The engraving to be found upon the balance bridge of watches as late as 1920 is a persistence of this originally Renaissance decoration.

Dials were either enameled or of engraved metal in the earliest English work. Later a sort of metal dial known as champlevé became common. In this, the figures were made to stand out upon a metal plate by engraving away the metal between the indications. The remaining base was matted. The white enamel dial was introduced soon after 1720 and gradually became the usual sort. Now that minute hands were universal, a white surface was much more practical. In many cases, the steel hands were nearly invisible against the champlevé silver background, particularly after it had become somewhat tarnished.

England stole another great march upon world watchmaking about 1700 when the art of jewelling the movement was developed. The use of pierced gem stones as wear-proof pivot holes for the arbors of a watch was a British secret for almost a century and contributed to the English supremacy. At first the jewelling was confined to the balance arbor, and the use of a decorative diamond for the exposed endstone at the center of the balance cock became usual for the best watches. Later, as greater precision became possible, the other arbors were jewelled, and in the case of eighteenth-century Liverpool work the jewels were made so excessively large as to be called Liverpool windows. The addition of wear-proof bearings to the English watch eventually stimulated the search for the ultimate in timekeeping and helped bring about enormous advances in precision.

"Modern" watchmaking began in about 1725, when George Graham perfected the cylinder escapement. This invention, which was essentially the application of the clock "dead beat" escapement to watches, was in use until only a few years ago. In principle, the cylinder worked as follows. Triangular teeth were raised above the surface of the escape wheel. These engaged a hollow cylinder which was actually the balance staff itself. As the staff rotated back and forth, the teeth entered and left a cut-out section of the cylinder. As the cut portion revolved and released the wheel, it delivered impulse to the balance. The cylinder was made of a tube of steel, and the escape wheel was usually brass. This led to serious wear of the cylinder, as the escape wheel, being soft, picked up and used hard bits of grit as cutting edges. Later, important makers such as the Ellicotts made the wheels of steel and lined the cylinder with a tube of ruby, thereby making the cylinder practically wear proof. The complications of manufacture were, however, so great that the ordinary artisan could not use such a method. The cylinder was the first step beyond the verge and was used concurrently with it, initially by Graham, and later by an increasing number of makers, including the Ellicotts and Graham's successors, Mudge and Dutton.

Another escapement which found considerable favor among later British watchmakers was known as the duplex. Basically a French invention, in its final form it was patented by a Mr. Tyrer in England toward the end of the eighteenth century. It used an escape wheel of peculiar form, with long teeth and with smaller raised projections on the band of the wheel. The balance staff supported an arm at right angles which, in the correct position, engaged the raised or impulse teeth. Below the impulse arm was a small roller with a narrow notch. The long teeth locked upon the roller until

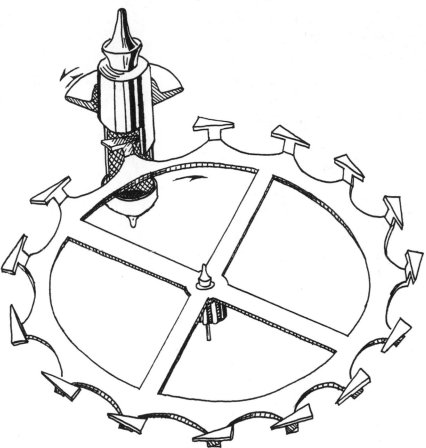

Fig. 8 Cylinder escapement

the rotation of the balance presented the notch to the locked tooth. It then slipped by, in the notch, and in the process the impulse arm was pushed by the raised tooth. The next locking tooth was then held by the roller until it could escape on the next revolution. This, then, received impulse in one direction only and was known as a single beat escapement. It was a difficult method to use, as the constructional details were most precise, but when well made and not worn badly, it was capable of extremely accurate results. It was used in precision pocket watches for more than fifty years.

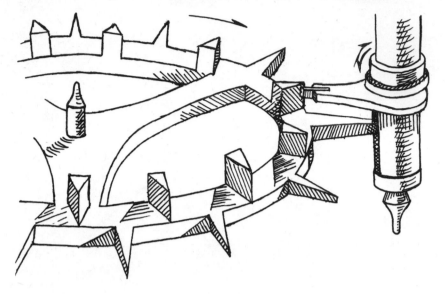

Fig. 9 Duplex escapement

In all of the watch escapements described thus far, the balance and its staff were never detached from the train of wheels. In the verge, the escape of one tooth implied the immediate arrest of the escape wheel by the next tooth. In the cylinder, the teeth were locked upon the staff or were escaping from it. In the duplex just described the same applied. In all of these, the locking was upon a moving part of the train, and was known as a frictional rest escapement.

The ideal, of course, was to produce an escapement which was completely detached from the influence of the train for as long as possible between the necessary cycles of impulse. Such an escapement would mitigate the adverse effect of friction during the lock and would, therefore, be less responsive to the inevitable variations of power. Much thought was given to this problem, and the solution which was most widely adopted for ordinary use was the invention of Thomas Mudge, an Englishman, about 1775. Mudge's escapement, known to us as the lever, has today supplanted all others.

It is a curious fact that Mudge never realized what he had accomplished. Admittedly, as he had designed it, it was more complex than

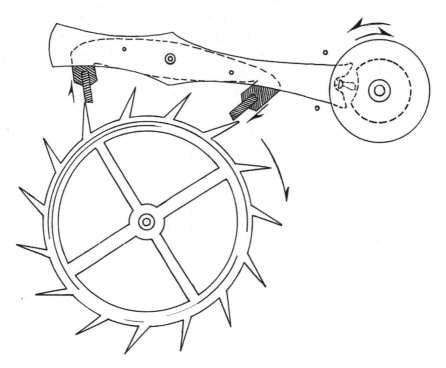

Fig. 10 Lever escapement

necessary and required considerable skill to construct, yet he put it aside after using it in only a few timepieces and showed little later interest in it.

In essence, the lever escapement used a wheel and pallets which were derived directly from the clock dead beat method of Mudge's old master, Graham. Whereas in the case of the clock the pallets furnished an impulse to the pendulum through a crutch, in the watch lever escapement the pallets held a long forked piece which was the lever proper. The balance staff held a circular roller, and from the surface of this roller, near its circumference, a pin projected vertically. The action was as follows: as the balance revolved, the pin ultimately entered the arms of the fork. When it did so, the force of its revolution pressed the fork aside, moving the pallets from their locked position on the escape wheel. Once the pallets were unlocked, the face of the pallet was forced up by the point of the wheel tooth as the wheel revolved, throwing the lever smartly to the other side. In this action the fork picked up the pin on the roller and threw it sharply in the same direction, delivering an impulse to the balance. Once the roller pin left the fork in this manner, it was free of any influence from the train and remained so until it entered the fork on its return trip and again unlocked and was impulsed in the opposite direction. This, then, was an escapement which was free, or detached, for a considerable portion of its action and delivered impulse at each turn of the balance in both directions. In order that the fork be prevented from moving so far to the side that it would be out of position to catch the pin on its return, banking pins were provided, arresting the travel of the lever. Two safety features were provided, so that the lever would not move away from the pins and unlock except when unlocked by the balance. First, a projection was mounted upon the lever, close to the fork. This projection, usually a vertically mounted pin in the earlier watches, would bear upon the roller if moved away from the banking pins. In order that the lever might cross over during unlocking and impulse, a small section of the roller was cut away, directly next to the impulse pin. The lever could not then get out of position, and could not move across except when the impulse pin was ready to receive impulse.

The next lever watches were made by a little group of London makers led by Josiah Emery during the years just preceding 1800. These watches were basically of the Mudge type, although some improvements were made. The number of lever watches made during these years was very small, and examples are rare and highly prized.

One defect of Mudge's safety action was the possible friction which the safety pin might produce if it were jolted away from the banking pins and contacted the roller. Variations in accuracy which puzzled some of the early makers probably were caused by this action. The solution was found by John Leroux of London about 1786. Leroux mounted his pallets in such a way that as the escape wheel tooth moved into the lock position, it was drawn by the angle of the pallet deeper into engagement. This "draw" held the pallet and lever safely

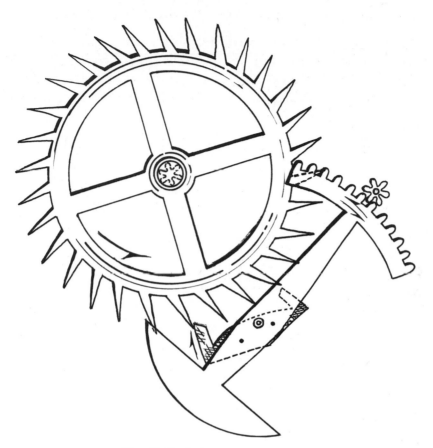

Fig. 11 Rack lever escapement

in position in all but the most catastrophic situations. It is still one
of the most important features of the modern lever watch.

By 1800 the lever escapement was not being made. It reappeared
in a different and less satisfactory form in Liverpool at about this
time, in a patent taken out by Peter Litherland. Litherland coupled
his lever to the balance staff through a toothed rack which engaged
a pinion on the staff itself. Actually, this "rack" lever had been invented by the Frenchman Hautefeuille in 1722, although it is evident that Litherland was not aware of the previous invention. This
escapement, although subject to wear, was rugged, and was made in
large numbers by Liverpool makers. It was superseded some twenty

years later by a variation in which the fork was used again and acted upon an impulse pin attached to a roller. The proportions of this "crank" roller were different from those of the Mudge type. The true lever escapement reappeared in perfected form in the middle 1820's and gradually took over the pre-eminence it has enjoyed to the present day.

While this book makes no attempt to treat other than English and American clock- and watchmaking, it is not possible to pass over the contributions of the Frenchman (originally Swiss) Abraham Louis Breguet. This man, who lived from 1747 until 1823, was undoubtedly the greatest watch- and clockmaker of all time (no pun intended). He stuck by the lever escapement in its pure form when England had seemed to have forgotten it, or at least seemed to be interested in more primitive forms such as the rack. It is probable that the reintroduction of the true lever in England was inspired by Breguet's exquisite work. He rarely made two watches exactly alike, so long as he felt that a change might be beneficial. Their value today, of course, is astronomical, and rightly so. Breguet's influence upon workmanship was immense, and we must be aware of his tremendous contribution. Like most great makers, he was widely faked, and the Breguet name on a watch may mean nothing.

Another advance in watch- and clockmaking made the accurate determination of longitude possible. The fact that England ruled the waves was due in no small part to the development of the marine chronometer, a feat which can be credited to English horology.

The proposal that a ship's longitude (one of the two necessary factors in the determination of position) could be ascertained by determining local time and comparing it with an accurate standard clock was first mentioned by Gemma Frisius in 1530. The degree of accuracy necessary was far beyond the reach of horology of the period, for it is necessary to keep a predictable rate within two or three seconds a day. When we remember that the best timepiece of 1530 might occasionally keep within fifteen minutes a day, we understand why this was only a theoretical solution. This was the case until the introduction of the pendulum and balance spring. Then, suddenly, the solution appeared possible.

As England and other great nations began to trade with newly discovered parts of the world, maritime disasters caused by imperfect calculation of ships' positions became all too common. It was the business of governments to take notice of this trend and to attempt to solve the longitude problem. In 1714 the British government offered an enormous reward for the production of a timekeeper which would determine longitude at sea within one degree and it proposed double the amount for one-half degree accuracy. This last offer of twenty thousand pounds was a fortune in 1714 and inspired many to attempt to win it. The award was won, not by a trained watch- or clockmaker, but by a self-taught genius who had begun his career as a Yorkshire carpenter. John Harrison (1693–1776) spent a lifetime in the pursuit of the prize, and by impeccable workmanship produced a timekeeper which in 1761 met the conditions set forth by the British crown. He became enmeshed in bureaucratic red tape in trying to collect, however, and it was not until 1773 that he received the last of the reward money. He died three years later. Curiously, only one of Harrison's achievements survived him. This, a method of keeping a timepiece going while it is being wound, or maintaining power, still exists in contemporary weight-drive regulator clocks.

Not the least of the problems which beset the really accurate marine timekeeper or "chronometer" was that of temperature compensation. Harrison was certainly aware of this problem and had invented a compensation pendulum for clocks which is still used. This invention took advantage of the difference in the degree of expansion of the metals brass and steel, and by balancing the difference through use of parallel rods of these metals, created a pendulum of practically invariable length under variations in temperature. This "gridiron" pendulum has been as popular as Graham's mercury pendulum.

Harrison attempted to use the gridiron principle in the first of his marine timekeepers, but the attempt was only partially successful. Later, in his "Number Four," which won the prize, he used a strip of brass and steel riveted together which bent one way and then the other under stress of temperature change, effectively altering the length of the balance spring and compensating—to a degree—for the changes in elasticity and length of the spring itself. He was well aware that a reasonably complete temperature compensation had to be made in the balance wheel itself, and so stated before his death. This was not accomplished in England until the time of Arnold and Earnshaw some twenty years later. Unknown to Harrison, the French artisan Pierre LeRoy (1717–1785) had made a completely successful marine chronometer in 1766 which did contain the compensation in the balance. LeRoy was another of the great French horologists who can be mentioned only in passing. His chronometer assures his greatness, although he, too, left little which later makers could use.

John Arnold (1736–1799) and Thomas Earnshaw (1749–1829) were London makers who lived through the genesis of the marine chronometer and saw it accepted for use during their lifetimes. Both were, in large part, responsible for the development of the chronometer as we know it today. From where we sit today, it is really impossible to determine which one was responsible for the invention of the chronometer "detent" escapement and the bimetallic compensation balance. These are the heart of the present-day marine timekeeper and, as presently used, are the production of Earnshaw. It appears, however, that the basic work on both should be equally credited to Arnold.

The development of the chronometer was again a search for a detached escapement. As finally realized, the train, through the escape wheel, was in contact with the balance staff only long enough for the wheel tooth to strike the impulse pallet and impart impulse, and this only in one direction. This left the balance completely unhindered by train irregularities, not only for the remainder of the impulse turn, but for the complete return rotation. Add to this the extreme precision of the chronometer train and the final form of

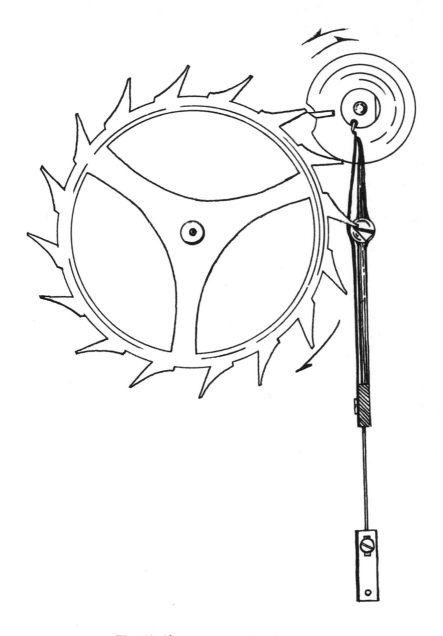

Fig. 12 Chronometer or detent escapement

Earnshaw's fused brass and steel balance for temperature compensation. The result was an instrument which, if well cared for, would meet the most stringent requirements for precision timekeeping at sea or ashore.

The action of the chronometer or detent escapement is as follows: A thin straight spring held the escape wheel motionless through a jewel pin or "locking stone" which was vertically mounted upon it. The balance staff had two rollers upon it, the larger of which carried an impulse pallet that registered with the wheel teeth. When the wheel was locked upon the spring detent, the impulse roller was free to pass between the wheel teeth. A smaller roller was also upon the balance staff, and this held a small pallet which registered with the spring detent. The detent was furnished at its tip with a weak spring. As the balance and staff revolved, the pallet on the small roller engaged the weak spring. It pressed the spring and the detent aside in one direction to pass, and in the process unlocked the wheel from the locking stone. When released, a wheel tooth would strike the impulse pallet on the staff and impart impulse. The wheel would then lock again on the detent, which had moved back into position after the small pallet had passed. When the balance and staff had completed the swing and begun to return in the opposite direction, the small pallet would engage the small spring on the detent, press it aside without disturbing the locking stone, and go on. In this way, the impulse was given in one direction only, and except for the impulse itself and the tiny contact with tne small spring on the return swing, the balance was completely detached from the train.

This is essentially the action of the Earnshaw refinement of the chronometer escapement. The extreme detachment of the balance made it potentially the best of all portable timekeeping escapements, and under good-to-excellent conditions it lived up to its potential. There were considerable numbers of pocket chronometers made in England during the 1800's, but the delicacy of the construction made it less suitable for pocket watches than the developed form of the lever. Watches of this chronometer type are reasonably rare and are much sought after today.

By 1860 in England the lever escapement had all but supplanted the other escapement forms. The lever itself underwent certain refinements, in both the form of pallets and escape-wheel teeth and the method of safety action. By this time the Swiss watch industry had begun to develop, and some of these achievements were Swiss-inspired. However, the lever had found its final form by the middle of the century, and the great changes which came about after this were in the methods of manufacture rather than in design.

It is both a tribute to British individuality and a sad commentary on English conservatism that a factory method of watch-or-clock-making never really developed, at least during the period of this study. As a matter of fact, when the industry finally realized that the American and Swiss manufacturing methods had taken away the world market, it was too late for England to recover her former leadership. The British hand methods produced some of the finest watches which the world has ever seen and continued to do so until the time of the First World War, but after about the middle of the 1800's it was a declining trade.

With a heritage like this, it is no wonder that the later American watchmaking industry reached a position of world leadership. Building upon the solid achievement of our English ancestors we developed factory methods which were practiced by some sixty companies. A few were immensely successful, others were short-lived. The best products of the best American companies were comparable to the best which any other nation ever produced.

3

Pennsylvania Clockmaking

CLOCK *making,* as such, did not exist in the earliest days of colonization of the New World. The earliest settlers brought time-keepers with them, and no doubt they did break or get out of kilter at times. The repair was probably entrusted to the locksmith (who was a very necessary part of society in the American Colonies) or, in cases of the inevitable tower or town clock, to the blacksmith, who was equipped to handle the large wheels and machinery of these great clocks. Aside from the town clocks, which were among the first timekeepers to be recorded, we have few records of clocks of the domestic type. The most affluent houses would certainly have had a lantern clock, English-made, and a few might have had a table or bracket clock or, in very rare cases, a tall clock. All of these would have been imported from the old country, and except for the lantern clocks, would have been found only in the most luxurious homes of the colonial governors. It was inevitable that the very earliest lantern clocks of the Virginia and New England settlers would be controlled by the balance wheel and would be of the most inaccurate type. Later, after 1660, when Huygens had invented the pendulum, a trade developed here in converting what few lanterns there were to the new controller. This, again, would be learned and practiced by the worker in wrought metals, either the locksmith or the blacksmith. In short, there were no clock *makers* in the earliest Colonial times. There just weren't enough clocks to support such a trade. Those who did fix clocks were primarily metalworkers in another field, and clockmaking was a sideline.

Generally speaking, clockmaking in the Colonies developed in two groups, or schools, if you wish. The Delaware Valley makers, from New York to Virginia and the Carolinas, tended to work in somewhat the same manner. Philadelphia, being the center of trade, produced a major number of clocks and clockmakers. The other school, centered in Boston, included all of New England. The two schools were of equal importance until approximately 1810, when the rise of the Connecticut industry began and ultimately destroyed the handmaking of clocks in this country.

For the purposes of this discussion, which is directed toward the collector of clocks, we will make only casual reference to the tower or public clocks. They were here in very early times, and some of the earliest references to individuals in the trade are found in the town or city records when such artisans were retained to build or to keep in repair a tower clock. But we are more interested here in the domestic clocks which were being produced by colonial makers.

To the author's knowledge, there are no examples of the true lantern clock made by a colonial craftsman. There are posted-frame movements which resemble lantern clocks in layout, but these were invariably made for use with a dial of the tall-clock type, never with the brass plate-within-the-frame of the lantern clock. These posted-frame clocks, which were quite early, showed the work of the English emigrant and were usually of a rather crude provincial style. Often they were simply hung upon the wall, as the original lantern clocks were, the pendulum wagging exposed below the dial. (This "wag-on-the-wall" type has persisted until the present day.) The colonial sorts, originally made with metal dials but later made with painted faces, were almost always of thirty-hour duration and wound by pulling the weight up on its chain. We cannot consider this type as being a cased clock, although frequently the movements were enclosed in a crude cover.

Historically, the Delaware Valley and its dependencies were dominated by British settlement. It is true that the Swedes, Germans, and Dutch were also involved, but they were eventually quite swamped in the cities. Only in the Pennsylvania hills did the German influence continue to predominate and affect clockmaking. It is obvious that the Pennsylvania clocks would show the styles which were current in England, just as the furniture styles did. The demand was generally for tall clocks, less for the English bracket clocks, although these were made in limited quantities. The bracket clock, being spring-driven, was a rather expensive article to manufacture in the Colonies, and could no doubt be more reasonably imported from the old country. (Some such imported clocks still exist in old families, documented as to the time of importation.) Tall clocks could be competitively made, and while they were at first only for the rich household, the demand increased as the financial fortunes of the colonists improved, until it was profitable for a man to take up the trade of clockmaking, although he made clocks only to order.

The earliest Delaware Valley tall clocks are exceedingly rare and are cased in the Queen Anne style: walnut, square brass and silvered brass dial, attached columns to the hood, narrow trunk, lenticle for sight of the pendulum bob, moulded or flat hood top, and small plinth. In general, this is what was being produced in the clock-making centers in England about 1700, although the colonial examples show the lack of detail and sophistication expected from provincial craftsmen. Such makers as Bispham, Cottey, and Peter Stretch were working in Philadelphia during this period, and their productions are as described.

About 1720 the English style for the arched top penetrated the Colonies, and cases made after this date usually incorporated this feature. At first, with the brass dial, the arch contained the maker's name and city inscribed upon a cartouche. Later the space was gen-

A PORTFOLIO
OF ILLUSTRATIONS

Ill. 1 The main dial of this typical European public clock has a variety of astronomical indications, as well as hands to indicate mean time. The structure to the right contains many automatons, with the figure at the top pulling wires to ring the bells. At the base a procession moves in and out of the doors as the striking occurs. It would seem that cities vied in the Middle Ages to produce the most complicated town clock.

Ill. 2 Sand glasses were once very popular timekeepers. This one is divided into four parts to indicate quarter-hours as well as the hour itself. This sort was often used in churches, where it was placed beside the pulpit. Turned at the beginning of the sermon, it would indicate to the clergyman periods shorter than one hour.

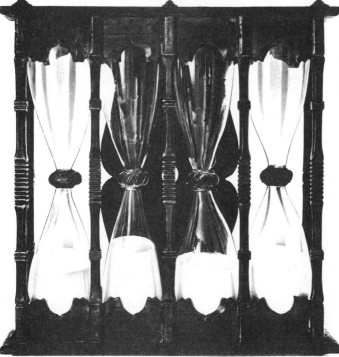

Ill. 3   The English chamber or lantern clock was the domestic timekeeper from approximately 1580 until the invention of the pendulum in 1660. This example, dated 1657, uses the ancient balance wheel and verge escapement. It shows many of the early signs. The hour or "chapter" ring is quite narrow, and the one hand is simple in design. The center dial is an alarm indicator. (Author's collection)

Ill. 4   The lantern clock has the time and striking trains of wheels arranged one behind the other, with the time in front. It was not until front winding, rather than rope pulling, became usual that trains were placed side by side. This picture shows the relatively primitive wheel work. The balance-wheel-controlled lantern was a capricious timekeeper, and the restriction to one hand and quarter-hour markings is an indication of its shortcomings.

Ill. 5 The English bracket or table clock in its purest form. The clock on the left is signed by Thomas Tompion with partner Edward Banger. Tompion was the top maker in England during the late seventeenth century. Both of these clocks date from about 1700.

Ill. 6 A fine example of a typical mid-eighteenth-century British bracket clock. In this case the arch dial has arrived, and the central quarter-hour markings have disappeared. The clock is signed by Normand MacPherson of Edinburgh, Scotland, and contains an extremely sophisticated movement. About 1760. (Author's collection)

Ill. 7 It is extremely difficult to decide how much clockmaking actually took place in Colonial America. Here we have three clocks which probably represent what we are likely to find. The bracket clock on the left is signed by Thomas Wagstaffe, a London Quaker who had many Philadelphia connections. The case is ebonized poplar and obviously of colonial manufacture. The movement and dial were probably brought to Philadelphia and cased there. About 1775.

The movement of the center clock was probably finished in Colonial America from imported parts. Its mahogany case is local. About 1800.

The clock on the right is signed on the dial by Robert Pearsall, New York. The movement, of great sophistication, is signed by Thomas Reid of London and dated 1796. The case seems to be of black lacquered cherry and is certainly a local production.

Here we see the combination of cases and movements available to Colonial and Federal buyers, as far as the bracket-clock style is concerned. This sort of clock is quite rare. (Author's collection)

Ill. 8   All of these tall clocks represent basic styles which were copied in this country. This one, with a cushion or bell top, represents the Queen Anne period and was made in England about 1710 by Mark Hawkins of St. Edmunds Bury. This style was usually made in walnut; its head was sometimes square rather than bell shaped.

Ill. 9 Chinese lacquer cases were common in England from 1700 until about 1760. This example was made by John Martin of London about 1700. The trunk door was restored in the distant past. The American clocks with lacquer are now rare.

Ill. 10 A typical English Chippendale case containing a movement signed by Lowery of Whitehaven. The woods are mahogany on pine. About 1760.

Ill. 11   A case in the Sheraton-Hepplewhite style. The woods are mahogany, holly, satinwood, and thuja. This would date from about 1780.

Ill. 12   A case in the Regency style of 1810. The movement was by Handley and Moore of London. The woods are mahogany on oak. (Author's collection)

Ill. 13 A superb example of Baroque magnificence in a British tall-clock dial, this one being Irish. The brilliance of the silvered chapter ring on the gilded dial plate is particularly effective. The seconds ring is inlaid in the plate, and the cast-brass spandrel ornaments are carefully chased. The engraving in the dial center is extraordinarily florid. About 1740.

My British friends, particularly those of the "nothing but London" school, may think this too elaborate. I personally admire this sort of provincial complication. (Author's collection)

Ill. 14   An excellent example of a very early colonial clock. This one, signed by Isaac Pearson, of Burlington, New Jersey, shows all of the characteristics of the Queen Anne style. An inscription inside the door reads: Made for Elisha Laurence, 1723. The case is walnut. (Courtesy, Henry Francis du Pont Winterthur Museum)

Ill. 15   This clock was made by Thomas Stretch, son of the pioneer maker Peter Stretch. The Stretches worked in Philadelphia from 1702 until 1765. This case, pure Queen Anne in style, was made about 1730. (Courtesy, H. and R. Sandor, Inc., Lambertville, New Jersey)

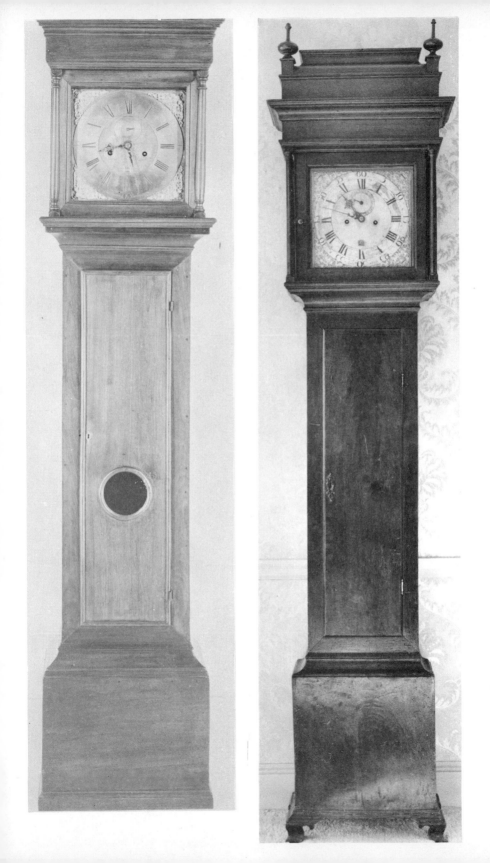

Ill. 16 Benjamin Rittenhouse who has been over-shadowed by his more famous brother David, made some outstanding pieces during his clockmaking career. This certainly qualifies as one of the best. It is a very fine example of the Chippendale styling, although the wood is walnut rather than the more usual mahogany. The proportions, from the ogee bracket feet to the scroll rosettes at the top, are faultless. About 1780. (Courtesy, George Winner, Philadelphia)

Ill. 17 This brass and silvered dial is in the best tradition of the English Baroque styling. The complications—center seconds, a calendar, and a tidal dial and moon phase in the arch—are most interesting to the collector. All of the dial pointers are delightful, but trying to decipher the time in dim light would be difficult.

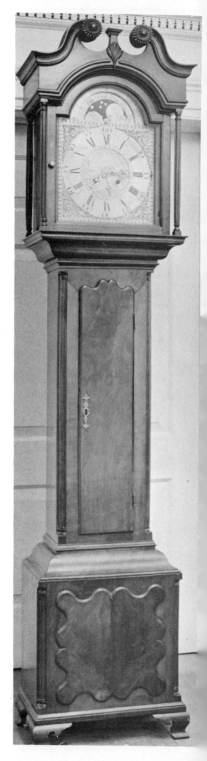

Ill. 18 This is one of the greatest clocks in the Philadelphia Chippendale tradition. The extremely elaborate hood carving combined with the richness of the highly figured mahogany give an effect unequalled save for very few examples. The maker, Edward Duffield, who may have been the successor to the Stretch family, was one of the greatest of the Philadelphia school. He was at work from 1750 until about 1775. He was a personal friend of Benjamin Franklin and acted as executor of his will. (Courtesy, Henry Francis du Pont Winterthur Museum)

Ill. 19   The Drexel Rittenhouse is universally regarded as the greatest American clock. Made by David Rittenhouse about 1772, it was sold in 1774 to Thomas Prior. After several ownerships it was given to the Drexel Institute in 1898 by Mrs. George W. Childs, and remains there today.

While the case had to be enormous to contain all of the complications, it is in the highest traditions of the Philadelphia Chippendale school and deserves to rank with the great antique highboys of Philadelphia. (Courtesy, Drexel Institute of Technology, Philadelphia)

Ill. 20   This closeup of the hood and dial of the Drexel Rittenhouse shows the exquisite elaboration of the casework and the complexity of the dial and movement. The array on the arch is an orrery showing the motions of the planets. The clock has center seconds, moon phase, date and month, quarter striking, astrological aspect, a choice of ten tunes to be played at the hour, and, of course, time of day. (Courtesy, Drexel Institute of Technology, Philadelphia)

Ill. 21 A delightful example of the country interpretation of the Chippendale style can be seen in this unsigned Pennsylvania clock. Although curly maple is not in itself unsophisticated, the wood does give a country look to the clock. The proportions, a somewhat shortened trunk and lengthened plinth, are pure "upstate." All in all, this case, with its exposed dovetails and "Dutch" rosettes, is a real beauty. About 1800. (Courtesy, Florene Maine, Antiques, Ridgefield, Connecticut)

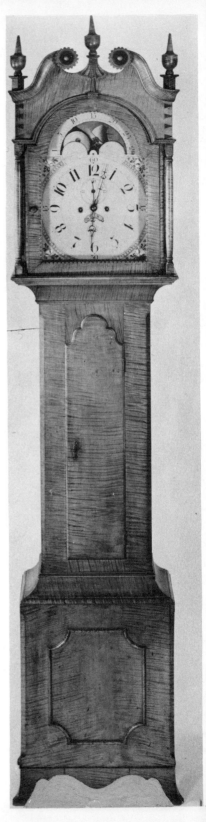

Ill. 22 This closeup of the dial and hood of the maple clock opposite shows the painted dial in detail. The painted dial should not be considered a poor relative of the brass dial, for in its period it was preferred to the "old-fashioned" metal one. The brightly colored spandrel paintings are enhanced by the country scalloping of the dial surround of the door. (Courtesy, Florene Maine, Antiques, Ridgefield, Connecticut)

Ill. 23 When the Hepplewhite-Sheraton styles arrived in the American Colonies after the Revolution, they were absorbed by and combined with the existing Chippendale to produce a clock such as this. Veneers and stringing lines are combined with quarter columns in the trunk and curly pediment in the hood. The panel below the trunk door is an Irish or North English usage which was carried over into the new Federal Union. See Illustration 11.

The clock is signed by George Jones, Wilmington, Delaware, although the case certainly looks like a Philadelphia production. It is a very handsome piece. About 1820. (Courtesy, Henry Francis du Pont Winterthur Museum)

Ill. 24 New Jersey produced its quota of tall-clock makers, and many of the Jersey products rank with the best, particularly in the Federal style. Joakim Hill was at work in the early 1800's and was a prolific maker. His cases were constructed by the best cabinetmakers. This one still has the label of John Scudder, Westfield, on the back of the trunk door. The design shows most of the Hepplewhite-Sheraton features and includes the Irish panel below the trunk door seen in Illustration 23. About 1815. (Courtesy, H. and R. Sandor, Inc., Lambertville, New Jersey)

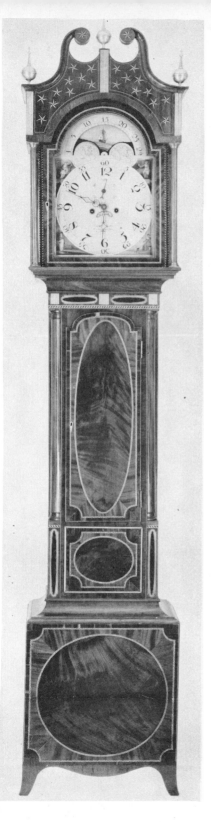

Ill. 25   The earliest clockcases made in New England would naturally be crafted in the Queen Anne style. This example was made by Gawen Brown, Boston, and dates from about 1750. Brown was at work during the second half of the eighteenth century and represents the beginning of what later became the Boston school. (Courtesy, Old Sturbridge Village, Massachusetts)

Ill. 26   The New England tall clock reached the pinnacle of development about 1810 with this sort by Simon Willard. This is the pure form of the Roxbury case; it is one of the most distinguished examples in existence. The fret on the top of the hood arch is the epitome of Roxbury styling.

On the right is a miniature (or "granddaughter") in the same style. It is a type which has become associated with the name of Joshua Wilder, of Hingham, who produced many of them. They are much sought after and are quite rare. (Courtesy, Old Sturbridge Village, Massachusetts)

Ill. 27 Simon Willard's greatest contribution to the design of the clock—case as well as movement—lies in his invention of the banjo. This name is relatively recent, and in Willard's own time, it was known only as the "patent timepiece." This is the pure form, with no gilding and with stylized designs on the glasses. About 1810. (Courtesy, Old Sturbridge Village, Massachusetts)

Ill. 28 The most elaborate development of the banjo idea was achieved by Lemuel Curtis, of Concord, Massachusetts, in this design known as the girandole. This specimen, dating from about 1815, is considered to be one of the most beautiful American clocks. Curtis was impeccable in his clockwork as well as his cases. Special note should be taken of the hands, which are frequently taken to be another Curtis aesthetic triumph. Actually this design was a standard British one, and appears on many English table clocks of the period. Curtis seemed to use this hand style to the exclusion of all others on his superb girandoles. (Courtesy, Old Sturbridge Village, Massachusetts)

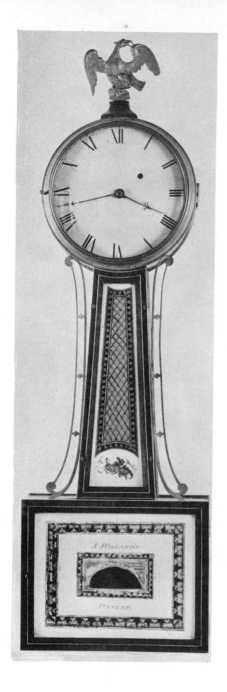

Ill. 29   The American lyre is a variant of the basic banjo style. This example is plainer than many, as some have painted glasses instead of the mahogany throat and box fronts. The type is attributed to Aaron Willard, who certainly made many of them. This one is unsigned, although the movement appears to be the same as those made by Abiel Chandler of Concord, New Hampshire. About 1830 (Author's collection)

Ill. 30   While all of these carry the name of the Philadelphia Riggs family, they are all by Edward Howard of Boston. The Riggs were agents for the Howard firm and sold many of the Howard products. These styles are all derived from the banjo. They are called, from left to right, the figure-eight, the Howard banjo, and the keyhole. (Author's collection)

Ill. 31 While this is a relatively late example of the English balloon-on-case clock, its predecessors may well have been the inspiration for the Massachusetts shelf clock, examples of which follow. This one, by Robert Wood of London, dates from about 1810, and is a spring fusee clock with a long pendulum beating in the lower case. This arrangement gives the advantage of a longer pendulum in a table-type case. (Author's collection)

Ill. 32 This is Simon Willard's earliest wall clock, which was obviously designed to be reasonably priced. It is weight-driven, since springs were very expensive in America. The style can safely be referred to as the balloon-on-case type shown in Illustration 31. The peculiar dial opening is referred to as the kidney dial and is an obvious attempt to give the feeling of the balloon without the expense of the balloon casework. The "feet" and the lower case make the suite a modest copy of the English style. The combination makes one of the most charming of all American types in its lack of sophistication. Willard was still working at the family farm in Grafton, Massachusetts, when this was made, about 1780. (Courtesy, Old Sturbridge Village, Massachusetts)

Ill. 33   This is a refinement of the wall clock shown in Illustration 32. Here the case has feet, for table or mantel use. The basic idea is the same, with the kidney dial and case-on-case design. The wood is, of course, mahogany. This is another clock signed Simon Willard, Grafton. It is obviously later than the preceeding example, but not by much. (Courtesy, Old Sturbridge Village, Massachusetts)

Ill. 34   Elnathan Taber, one of Simon Willard's apprentices, made this specimen; it is a stylistic development of the types shown before. The kidney dial remains, but the pseudo clock-on-case has disappeared, and the two parts are fused into one. The Sheraton influence is strong here in the highly figured mahogany and stringing lines. In all of these a simple time movement was used, quite similar to the patent banjo type. About 1810. (Courtesy, Old Sturbridge Village, Massachusetts)

Ill. 35   This clock, signed by Daniel Balch Jr., Newburyport, Massachusetts, is an extraordinary variant of the Massachusetts shelf style as developed by the Roxbury makers. The case is a mixture of styles, and shows an original approach to the basic design of the Willards. While Simon went into the banjo, Aaron continued to refine the style, and variants such as this were made by subsidiary "schools" like the one at Newburyport. It included David Wood, also of Newburyport, and William Fitz, of Portsmouth, New Hampshire. This case shows a further fusing of the two parts, and the kidney dial has at last been dropped. About 1810. Time and strike. (Courtesy, Henry Francis du Pont Winterthur Museum)

Ill. 36   The last stage in the development of the Massachusetts shelf clock. The design, distinctly American, is at last a unit, and the top and bottom are faced with reverse-painted glass panels. The dial is dished (concave), a cheaper means of creating an effect similar to the British convex (or "boom") dials, a type which was not being made in this country at the time. The hands of this specimen are typical Willard. The clock is signed by Aaron Willard and dates from about 1825. (Author's collection)

Ill. 37 The genesis of the Connecticut wooden-clock industry may be seen in this clock, Eli Terry's earliest production model, the box. This particular specimen was made by Seth Thomas under rights sold to him by Terry. The movement is contained between wood straps and is a rack striker. The entire clock, hands and all, is behind the glass door, which is reverse-painted with the dial and spandrel ornaments. The pendulum is off center. This is one of the rarest American clocks, and the predecessor of the pillar and scroll. About 1816. (Courtesy, Old Sturbridge Village, Massachusetts)

Ill. 38 Within a year or two, Terry had refined the box (Illustration 37) into the pillar and scroll shown here. The style follows the Sheraton-Hepplewhite lead and is an example of designing genius. While this has become known as the Terry style, there is no evidence that Terry was responsible for the case. Terry patented the movement and the case may just have developed as a joint effort in the Terry firm. This specimen shows the outside escapement stage in the development of the Terry wood movement. About 1817. (Courtesy, Old Sturbridge Village, Massachusetts)

93

Ill. 39 The clock on the left shows the final stage in the pillar and scroll design. This clock was signed by Charles Kirk of Bristol, Connecticut and dates from about 1828. The specimen on the right is an example of the transition case showing the Hitchcock and Empire influences. By Ephraim Downs, Bristol, Connecticut, about 1830. Both have Terry-type wooden movements. (Author's collection)

Ill. 40 Chauncey Jerome's design of the bronzed looking-glass clock revolutionized the Connecticut clock industry in the 1830's. The clock shown on the right is one of Jerome's clocks. This style drove the pillar and scroll from the scene. The clock on the left is in the same style by Seth Thomas, Plymouth. Both about 1832. (Author's collection)

Ill. 41 The revolution caused by Jerome's looking-glass clock opened the
way for other Empire influences. This pair shows the Empire carved columns
and splats at the head. Some of the carving on such clocks is remarkably fine.
The clock on the left is an example of late Empire by Ephraim Downs. The
one on the right is by Williams, Orton, and Preston, Farmington, Connecticut.
(Author's collection)

Ill. 42 The Empire case styles gradually became somewhat heavier as the clock on the left shows. It has an eight-day brass-weight movement by Forrest-ville Manufacturing Company, Connecticut. The one on the right is by Spencer, Hotchkiss and Company, of Salem Bridge. The Salem Bridge clock contains the brass eight-day movement developed by Heman Clark. Both about 1830. (Author's collection)

Ill. 43 A few makers in the East fought the trend toward mechanization and mass production. Their products were superb, but their careers were financial failures. This clock, by Silas Burnham Terry, Eli's son and the genius of the family, is a masterful piece of handwork. "S. B." deserves recognition as one of the great American clockmakers. About 1830. (Author's collection)

Ill. 44 These clocks show the last evidence of a proud tradition, the Pennsylvania clock. When the market was flooded with the cheap Connecticut products, the Pennsylvania tall clock was priced out of the market. A few makers attempted to stem the tide and make clocks which would compete. They were doomed to failure, for their tradition of handicraft and heavy brass movements could not match the cheap stampings and machine finishing of the Yankee clocks. Both of these specimens contain scaled-down cast-brass and hand-finished grandfather movements. The one on the left is by Sam Solliday, Doylestown, Pennsylvania and contains a thirty-hour movement. Dated February 21, 1837. The other is by his brother George Solliday at Montgomeryville and contains an eight-day movement. About 1837. (Author's collection)

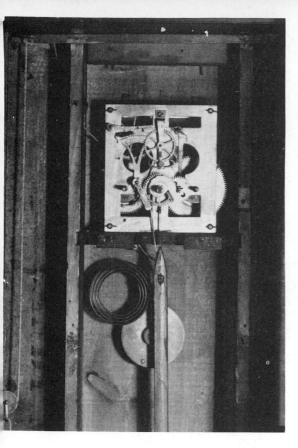

Ill. 45 The interior of the clock shown on the left in Illustration 40. The movement is the standard Terry type, and the makers "paper" pasted in the back is in unusually fine condition. (Author's collection)

Ill. 46 The interior of the clock shown on the right in Illustration 42. This is the Salem Bridge movement which is not common in Connecticut clocks. As can be seen, it is a rack striker. (Author's collection)

Ill. 47 The first of the American spring movements, and a breakthrough for the Connecticut industry. This design, made under the E. C. Brewster label, probably was created by Charles Kirk. The brass springs are contained in stationary barrels that are part of a cast-iron back plate. It is a rack striker. The movement is in its original case, one made for a weight movement. About 1840. (Author's collection)

Ill. 48　The ubiquitous ogee (or O.G.) case was derived from the popular mirror or picture-frame moulding of the period. At first the moulding was flat, as in the center clock by Chauncey Boardman. It probably dates from about 1844 and is an example of a very late wooden thirty-hour movement. The curly maple, walnut, and mahogany clock on the left is by Boardman and Wells and shows the true wave-like ogee moulding. About 1840. The Boardman enterprises were based in Bristol. The clock on the right is signed by Hiram Welton, who for a short time was the successor to the Terry enterprises. The movement of this clock was designed by Eli Terry for Welton to circumvent the Jerome patent. (Author's collection)

Ill. 49　The text covers the career and inventions of Joseph Ives, another of the real American geniuses. Not the least of his inventions was the "wagon spring" power plant for his brass movements. The wagon spring can be seen at the base of the case; it is not wound. The ends of the spring are raised in winding, and the power in the flexure is coupled to the wheels by a series of levers and lines. This is a case-on-case steeple clock. About 1845. Made under the Ives patents by Birge and Fuller of Bristol. (Courtesy, Old Sturbridge Village, Massachusetts)

Ill. 50   This illustration and Illustration 51 must be looked at together. The Gothic influence in England accompanied the Chippendale style and continued through the Regency period into the early Victorian period. The three English clocks shown here all date from about 1820 and are variants of the lancet window style. The center one contains elaborate moon work on the dial and is a chimer on ten bells. The clock is signed by Ellicott and Taylor, but it actually was made by Thwaites and Reed. The clock on the right is a mixture of Chippendale Gothic and Thomas Hope influences. The hands are the "Curtis" style mentioned in the girandole illustration. All three of these clocks are predecessors of the American Gothic styles. (Author's collection)

Ill. 51   Although the Gothic influence on furniture design had continued in England since about 1770, it did not reach America until the 1840's. The steeple designs in our clocks are often claimed as inventions of Elias Ingraham of Bristol, but he merely created an American form of the English designs. The curly maple beehive on the left is by Brewster and Ingraham of Bristol. The ripple front Gothic in the center is by J. C. Brown of Bristol. The clock on the right is the standard steeple and is by Brewster and Ingrahams. All of these are about 1845. (Author's collection)

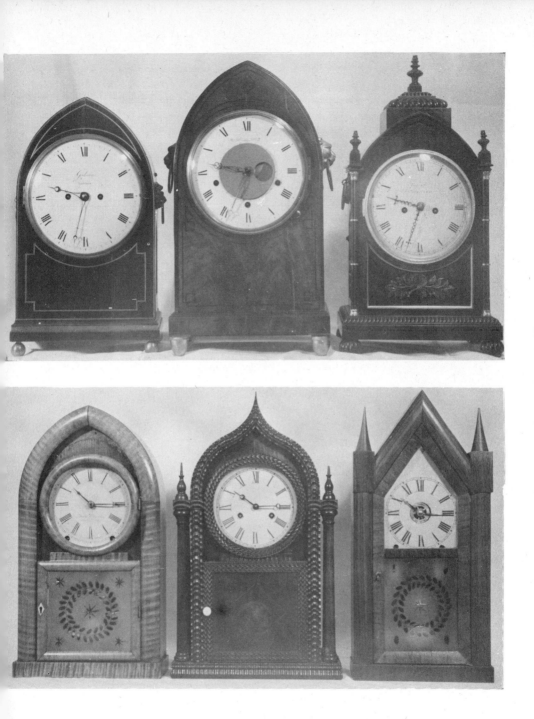

Ill. 52   The advent of the coiled-steel driving spring about 1850 caused an incredible proliferation of case forms. The fall of weights had required certain case styles, but now the spring drive allowed a mass of styles; those shown here are perhaps among the most satisfactory. The rounded or angularly rounded top cases were popular for fifty years or more. From left to right: E. Ingraham and Company, Seth Thomas, Plymouth Hollow (with S. T. hands), and Gilbert Manufacturing Company, Winsted, Connecticut, 1860–1875. (Author's collection)

Ill. 53   Connecticut makers had been experimenting with various sorts of "marine" movements since the days of the Terrys. Finally a crude type of watch "lever" escapement movement was standardized by most makers and applied where pendulums could not be used. These were advertised for steamships, locomotives, etc. The small one on the left is by S. B. Jerome, New Haven, Connecticut, and has a thirty-hour movement. About 1860. The larger one is by Seth Thomas, and has a double-spring eight-day movement. About 1880. (Author's collection)

Ill. 54 The clock known as the Connecticut regulator comes in many sizes. Originally derived from the English dial types used for offices, etc., it soon developed typically American forms. This one, signed by Seth Thomas, Plymouth Hollow, is the earliest form of the Seth Thomas Number 3 Regulator. This movement was designed and possibly made by Silas Burnham Terry for Seth Thomas, and has a weight-driven dead-beat escapement of regulator-quality and a maintaining-power movement with a striking train. This movement rarely appears in clocks by S. B. Terry and Henry Terry. The case style is standard for the type, although later interpretations were not so detailed. The lower door has a reversed ogee moulding. About 1850. (Author's collection)

Ill. 55 The small Connecticut regulator or schoolhouse clock has had an extremely long run of popularity. This is an early example by E. N. Welch Manufacturing Company made about 1865. The Connecticut regulator became known as a drop octagon and is immensely popular today as a decorator's accent. (Author's collection)

Ill. 56 The American mass-produced perpetual calendar clock is another particularly Yankee type. This not only corrects automatically for the short months, but provides the 29th day for February in Leap Year. The clock on the left is by the Ithaca (N.Y.) Calendar Clock Company, which produced many between 1865 and 1914. About 1880. The one on the right is made according to the patent of one Fleichtinger, of Sinking Spring, Pennsylvania, and is one of the rarer styles. About 1890. (Author's collection)

Ill. 57 Seth Thomas, along with most of the other big companies, manufactured perpetual calendar clocks. This is one of their earlier ones. About 1880. (Author's collection)

Ill. 58 Another Seth Thomas, the standard sort which appeared in many business offices. These are still very handy to have in the modern household. About 1910. (Author's collection)

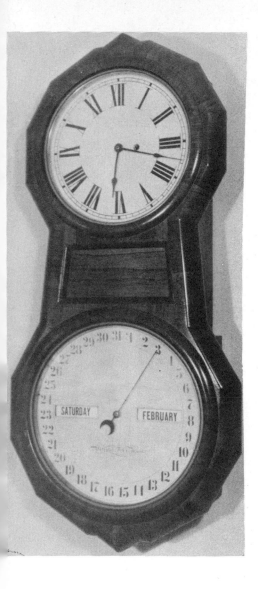

Ill. 59 & 60 Aaron Crane's invention of the torsion pendulum clock has been covered in the text. This specimen is not of the rarer month or year variety, but works on the same principle. It is weight-driven for a week on one winding, and the weights are measured in ounces instead of pounds. The three-ball "pendulum" which twirls at the end of the long thin spring can be clearly seen. The mechanical principle which couples the rotary motion of the three balls to the mechanism is most ingenious but not very efficient mechanically. The net result makes the clock delightfully capricious as a timekeeper. About 1840. (Author's collection)

Ill. 61 The marine chronometer was always an English rather than an American specialty. This specimen, signed by Louis Scherr and Company, Philadelphia, shows all the signs of British manufacture. It was probably made by Parkinson and Frodsham of London and Liverpool and the local name put on the dial for sale over here. In any case, chronometers signed by Philadelphia makers are rare. About 1845. (Author's collection)

Ill. 62 The watches shown here are all of Liverpool, England, manufacture. The design of the movements, the window jewelling, and the general feeling all say Liverpool. The center movement is signed by a Liverpool maker, but the other two are signed by "makers" in the United States. The watch on the left is marked S. and E. Roberts, Trenton, New Jersey, and the one on the right O. E. Sibley, Canandaigua, New York. The Canandaigua watch has an English hallmarked case dated 1816. The author is intrigued with what kind of market could have existed for a quality watch such as this in an outpost in New York State in 1816. The Trenton watch is not in its original case so cannot be dated accurately. Probably about 1835. These are characteristic of the watches available in this country from 1810–1850. (Author's collection)

Ill. 63 True American colonial watches are very rare. Whether they were actually "made" in the real sense here or imported complete and signed is unimportant. Even in England in the period 1770–1810 watches were finished by a maker from rough parts or blanks. The quality of the finished piece depended on the quality of the finishing. Such colonial watches as these may well have been finished from imported parts by local craftsmen. Since they had been trained in the English tradition, their watches would be indistinguishable from British products, and these are. Starting at top left, the makers are: David Townsend, Boston, 1801; and Ephraim Clarke, Philadelphia, 1797. The next row: Jacob Alrichs, Wilmington, Delaware, 1802; another by the same maker, 1797; and Thomas Parker, Philadelphia, 1796. The bottom row: Leslie and Price, Philadelphia, 1794; and Robert MacDowell, Philadelphia, 1798. (Author's collection)

Ill. 64 Two of the watches shown in Illustration 63. The 1802 Alrichs is at the top, and the Ephraim Clarke is at the bottom. Both are silver pair-case verge watches with dust covers. The Clarke boasts a large diamond endstone on the balance cock. Both have watch repair "papers" in the outcases, of Sam and George Solliday, who made fine Pennsylvania clocks. (Author's collection)

Ill. 65   The products of the American mechanized watch industry are characterized by the following pages from a catalogue of the 1880's. This page, showing the range of prices of Waltham 18 size movements, uncased, proves the width of the field covered. From the Vanguard at $70 to Number 1 at $8, there was no need that could not be filled. All of these were good, and the best were excellent.

AMERICAN WALTHAM WATCH COMPANY'S MOVEMENTS.

Gents' 18 Size, Full Plate, Stem-wind, Open Face or Hunting.

Nickel, 21 extra fine ruby jewels in raised gold settings double roller, exposed pallets, embossed gold patent micrometric regulator. compensation balance in recess, adjusted to temperature, isochronism and position, patent safety barrel, exposed winding wheels, patent Breguet hair spring hardened and tempered in form, elaborately finished nickel plates with gold lettering, plate and jewel screws gilded, steel parts chamfered, double sunk dial. The Vanguard is the finest 18 size movement in the world.

Vanguard.....................$60 00
Vanguard, non-magnetic 70 00

Nickel, 17 ruby jewels in gold settings, compensation balance, adjusted to temperature, isochronism and position, patent regulator, patent Breguet hair spring. hardened and tempered in form, fine glass enamel double sunk dial, the finest full plate movement in the world.

Crescent Street................ ....$40 00
Crescent Street, non-magnetic....... 50 00

Nickel, 17 ruby jewels in gold settings, compensation balance, adjusted to temperature, isochronism and position, patent regulator, patent Breguet hair spring, hardened and tempered in form, double sunk dial.

No. 35.....................$32 00

17 jewels (settings), compensation balance, adjusted to temperature, isochronism and position, patent regulator, patent Breguet hair spring, hardened and tempered in form, damaskeened, double sunk dial.

No. 25. Gilded..........................$24 00

NO EXTRA CHARGE FOR FANCY DIALS ON ANY GRADES, EXCEPTING 6 AND 0 SIZE, 7 JEWELS. FOR FANCY DIALS ON THESE TWO GRADES, 70 CENTS EXTRA.

17 ruby jewels, compensation balance, 5 pairs settings, patent regulator, hardened Breguet hair spring, double sunk dial, adjusted to heat, cold and position.

Appleton, Tracy & Co., 17 jewels, nickel.....................$32 00
Appleton, Tracy & Co., 17 jewels, gilt, damaskeened.................. 28 00
Appleton, Tracy & Co., 15 jewels, gilt 18 00

Compensation balance, 17 jewels in settings, patent regulator hardened Breguet hair spring, adjusted, double sunk dial.

P. S. Bartlett. Gilt.....................$16 00
P. S. Bartlett. Nickel.................. 18 00

17 jewels (settings), compensation balance, adjusted, patent regulator, patent Breguet hair spring, hardened and tempered in form, double sunk dial.

No. 87. Nickel...... ....$18 00
No. 85. Gilt.............................. 16 00

15 jewels (settings), compensation balance.

No. 83. Nickel $12 00
No. 81. Gilt 11 00

15 ruby jewels (settings), compensation balance, adjusted to temperature, isochronism and position, patent regulator, patent Breguet hair spring, hardened and tempered in form, double sunk dial.

No. 40. Non-magnetic, nickel $32 00
Non-magnetic, gilt....... ...... 25 00

Compensation balance, gilt, 7 jewels.

No. 1. Stem wind.....................$ 8 00
Non-magnetic..................... 10 00

119

Ill. 66   The Illinois Watch Company at Springfield produced a range of movements led by the famous Bunn Special of railroad fame.

Ill. 67   The best watches of their time in this country were certainly those of E. Howard and Company, Boston. The company produced only quality movements, none of them cheap, and the best were expensive indeed. Number 10, at $200 uncased, was the quality leader. As the catalogue states, the production of Howard movements was limited, and consequently quality never suffered. A Howard watch could actually rival a watch made anywhere in the world by line-production methods.

ILLINOIS WATCH COMPANY'S MOVEMENTS, SPRINGFIELD, ILL.

18 Size, Stem-Wind, Hunting and Open Face. Open Face are Lever Set.

Bunn Hunting or Open Face.	**No. 50.**	**I. W. Co.**

Bunn Hunting or Open Face.

Nickel, adjusted to temperature, isochronism and positions, 21 fine ruby jewels in gold settings, compensation balance with gold screws, patent regulator, Breguet hair spring, double sunk glass enamel dial.
Bunn Special $46 00

Nickel, adjusted to temperature, isochronism and positions, 17 ruby jewels in gold settings, compensation balance with gold screws, patent regulator, Breguet hair spring, double sunk glass enamel dial.
Bunn. Nickel $32 00
Bunn. Gilt, same as above. 28 00

Nickel, adjusted to temperature, isochronism and positions, 17 jewels (5 pairs in settings), compensation balance, patent regulator, Breguet hair spring, double sunk dial.
No. 65 .... $24 00

Half nickel, 17 jewels (5 pairs in settings), compensation balance, patent regulator, Breguet hair spring, double sunk dial.
No. 61 .... $16 00

Gilt, 17 jewels (5 pairs in settings), compensation balance, patent regulator, Breguet hair spring, double sunk dial.
No. 60 .... $15 00

Half nickel, 15 jewels (4 pairs in settings), compensation balance, patent regulator, Breguet hair spring.
No. 51 .... $13 50

Gilt, 15 jewels (4 pairs in settings), compensation balance, patent regulator, Breguet hair spring.
No. 50 .... $11 50

Half nickel, 11 jewels, compensation balance, patent regulator.
No. 99 .... $10 50

Half nickel, 11 jewels, compensation balance.
No. 101 .... $10 00

Gilt, 11 jewels, compensation balance.
No. 2 .... $9 50

Gilt, 7 jewels, compensation balance.
I. W. Co $8 00

Same as above, key winding.
I. W. Co $7 00

HOWARD WATCH COMPANY'S MOVEMENTS.

Hunting and Open Face, Stem Wind and Pendant Set. We Carry a Full Line of Solid Gold, Gold Filled, Silver and Silveroid Cases to Fit these Movements.

18 Size. Hunting and Open Face.	**14 Size. Open Face only.**	**16 Size. Hunting and Open Face.**

18 Size. Hunting and Open Face.

No. 1. 15 ruby jewels, Hunt'g only, gilt. $35 00
No. 2. Patent regulator, gilt 46 20
No. 3. Patent regulator, adjusted to heat and cold, gilt 57 40
No. 4. Patent regulator, nickel 63 00
No. 5. Patent regulator, adjusted to heat and cold, nickel 74 20
No. 6. Patent regulator, adjusted to heat, cold, position and isochronism, gilt. 85 40
No. 7. Patent regulator, adjusted to heat, cold, position and isochronism, nickel. 105 00
No. 8. 17 jewels, adjusted to temperature and isochronism, patent regulator, nickel. 140 00
No. 10. 17 jewels, adjusted to temperature, isochronism and positions, patent regulator, nickel 200 00

14 Size. Open Face only.

No. 4. 15 jewels, gilt .... $ 63 00
No. 5. 15 jewels, nickel, adjusted. 74 20
No. 7. 15 jewels, nickel, adjusted. 105 00

Our stock of Howard Movements is
limited but we will endeavor
to fill all Orders
Satisfactorily.

16 Size. Hunting and Open Face.

No. 2. Patent regulator. $46 20
No. 3. Patent regulator, adjusted to heat and cold 57 40
No. 4. Patent regulator, nickel 63 00
No. 5. Patent regulator, adjusted to heat and cold, nickel 74 20
No. 6. Patent regulator, adjusted to heat, cold, position and isochronism, gilt. 85 40
No. 7. Patent regulator, adjusted to heat, cold, position and isochronism, nickel. 105 00
No. 8. 17 ruby jewels, adjusted to temperature and isochronism, patent regulator, nickel. 140 00
No. 10. 17 ruby jewels, adjusted to temperature, isochronism and positions, nickel. 200 00

erally used for some astronomical indication such as the phases of the moon or, in rare cases in this area, a simple automaton, such as a rocking ship. The latter was usually a New England device. In almost all cases the tall clocks of the period showed seconds on a dial below the numeral twelve and, in many, the date in an aperture below the center post. It is amusing that many people today consider date indication to be of recent invention. Actually it is an ancient indication and of relatively simple mechanical achievement.

In order to appreciate the extraordinary flowering of the Philadelphia school of furniture making in the period after 1740 it is necessary to appreciate the fact that Philadelphia was founded in the middle 1680's by a wealthy leisure class which was used to luxury. By 1710 a considerable quantity of furniture was being made, and by 1740 a style had begun to evolve. The overseas influences were probably as much the Irish interpretations of the London styles as the London styles themselves, accenting rather elaborate carving of the hoods and the now detached hood columns. This while still using walnut as the case wood. The Quaker influence produced many cases in a somewhat more somber style.

It must not be forgotten that there was always a considerable import business in clocks. We often find entire movements and dials signed by English makers and cased here. We also find English-made-and-signed movements with dials made and signed locally, in local cases. The trade used any rational means to make sales, and I am sure that the result was, in any of the three situations, exactly what the customer bought: good timekeeping. He was not concerned with the antique authenticity which concerns us. In Philadelphia one still finds clocks where the movements were made by the English Quaker Thomas Wagstaff, who was active in London from 1760 to 1794. Almost all of these are in cases made either in Philadelphia or Newport, Rhode Island, where there were Quaker settlements. It is a matter of record that Philadelphia Quakers lodged with Wagstaff when in London, and it is entirely possible that a Wagstaff movement might accompany them home. The author is aware that the statement has been made that Wagstaff at one phase in his career had a store in Philadelphia as an outlet for his work, probably for his movements, cased locally.

As Philadelphia developed into a center of world trade, it became attractive to cabinetmakers from all parts of the British Isles. They came in some numbers and brought with them the latest styles, both in decoration and construction. The influences of Chippendale's *The Gentleman and Cabinet Maker's Director* (1754) and Ince and Mayhew's *System of Household Furniture* (1762) showed clearly in the development of the Philadelphia "Chippendale" style in furniture. Both of these style books were filled with suggested furniture forms in the English Rococo, and Philadelphia was not far behind London in adopting the newest fashion. The sophistication attained by the Philadelphia craftsmen was unique in the Colonies. The highest development of the style, in chairs and the unparalleled high- and lowboys, is well known to any student of American furniture. All of this had a direct bearing upon clock cases, which were made by the same group of men who were responsible for the Philadelphia developments.

A major change, of course, was the introduction of mahogany as a case wood. Until about 1740 almost all important tall clock cases were walnut; after this time, mahogany played an increasingly important part in the trade. It is true that walnut was never completely replaced in Philadelphia, and price books quoted both woods throughout the entire pre-Revolutionary period. Mahogany became, however, the stylish wood.

As houses became larger, tall clock cases became taller to fit the larger rooms and higher ceilings, and dials enlarged to fit the cases. Whereas earlier dials rarely exceeded ten by fourteen inches, they now became commonly twelve by sixteen and, not infrequently, thirteen by eighteen. The classic brass and silver dial with baroque spandrel ornaments was sometimes replaced by a simple engraved silvered brass plate, this being especially popular with the somber Quaker cases. Where the classic style was retained, the spandrels were filled with ornaments of rococo form, which were often a series of rather meaningless scrolls. Hands became standardized and during the Chippendale period exhibited the usual serpentine minute hand with a pierced hour hand.

The greatest stylistic change was made in the design of the hood. The earlier cases showed either a flat top, the rounded moulding of the Queen Anne, or, somewhat later, an arch conforming with the arch of the dial. The commonest Chippendale influence became the scroll modification of the broken pediment which today seems to be the only antique clock case style to the lay person. Some of these cases are great masterpieces of Philadelphia cabinetmaking. The famous Rittenhouse clock in the Drexel Institute in Philadelphia, the magnificent Duffield and the Wagstaff in a Philadelphia case owned and exhibited by Winterthur Museum in Wilmington, Delaware, are supreme examples of the type. Fine clocks of this sort are not often available to collectors today. Fortunately there are other simpler clocks and cases which will satisfy those of us who are interested in this phase of the hobby.

While the greatest influence in Philadelphia was certainly English, the large colony of Germans who settled in suburban Germantown and as far west as Lancaster was adapting the Chippendale to its own uses. The Bachman family of cabinetmakers, who constructed tall cases for movements made in Lancaster, worked in the Chippendale style, which, while heavier than the more sophisticated Philadelphia makers' work, deserves to be ranked with the best.

About 1780 the English style for the painted rather than metal dial became the Pennsylvania fashion, and from this time on the metal dial was restricted to the most expensive pieces. Dial painting became a trade, and the discerning collector can distinguish dials painted by the same hand for different makers.

In 1700 a clockmaker was restricted to real raw materials—brass, steel, and iron—in his work. By 1780 he had developed a brisk trade in parts from English sources. A very special clock might still be made from "scratch," but the usual clock was made with wheels and pinions cut from imported blanks or even from movements imported in their entirety. It is almost certain that decorative details such as hands and spandrel ornaments for brass dials were imported, and in some later clocks, painted dials are found with English marks of manufacture. It takes educated guesswork in many cases to determine what was made, what was "finished," and what was used as imported in colonial clocks.

The Colonies were at war with England when the classical styles of Hepplewhite and Sheraton began to influence English cabinet-making. During this important period there was no communication between the two countries. When the war was finally over, the new styles came to Philadelphia and the southern settlements in mature form. The result was an almost immediate lightening of tall-case design and the use of highly figured veneer panels and inlay in place of carving. While the "Chippendale" scrolled pediment continued, together with the use of quarter columns in the trunk, the trunk door and the face of the plinth were most often inlaid with oval lines of satinwood and panels of mahogany, the wood being finished to an extremely high luster. Dials were almost always painted, the spandrel corners showing fruit, flowers, sometimes abstract designs, and—rarely—depictions of the four seasons. Hands became light openwork designs in which the minute indicator was usually a longer form of the hour hand.

A movement complication which became fashionable after 1770 was the "center" seconds indication, the seconds hand being driven from the center of the dial and sweeping the entire dial circle. In some cases a center date indicator was used as well, making four hands radiate from the center post. While this was no doubt a saleable set of complications, it did little to make time-telling easier. Such a nest of pointers was almost indecipherable in poor light.

During this period of classical influence some particularly fine pieces were made in the outlying areas of the Philadelphia school. The Alrich family and George Jones in Wilmington, Delaware; the upstate Pennsylvania makers Jacob Eby and Jacob Hostetter, the Hoffs of Lancaster, Isaac Brokaw in Bridgeton, New Jersey; the Johnsons of Hagerstown, Maryland; John McKee of Chester, South Carolina; and many others made clocks which are worthy of the most serious consideration. The basic case woods were generally mahogany with satinwood or similar inlay, although cherry and curly maple did appear with some frequency.

The shelf clock never had much popularity in Philadelphia and its dependencies. The true bracket clock was made in small numbers, and a larger quantity was imported, either as completely cased examples or as movements and dials for casing here. The author has seen examples of British-made movements and probable British cases, with a Philadelphia maker's name engraved upon the back plate and dial. Again we are hard put to decide which are authentically American and which imports. The quality of workmanship in the movements which were locally made rarely equals that in the English movements. In the matter of bracket cases, the secondary woods are a fair guide, as well as the somewhat less sophisticated proportions of the locally made products, which were not usually embellished with much cast brass ornament.

The primary difficulty which the local maker faced in the production of the bracket clock was in procuring good springs. There was no manufacture of clock springs in this country, and importation was expensive. The movements themselves offered difficulties, such as the making of fusees, which required specialized equipment as well as techniques. The small clock never "caught on" with the consumer in Pennsylvania until the entry of the cheap Connecticut clocks of the 1820's and later, which dispensed with the fusee.

When Connecticut began to flood the area with cheap but serviceable products, the Pennsylvania tall clock industry died. There were attempts on the part of local makers to meet the competition by the production of weight-driven shelf clocks in the Connecticut style, but the local men had been too well trained, and the quality which they built into their clocks made them too expensive to compete. Jacob Custer of Norristown, Samuel and George Solliday of Doylestown and Montgomeryville, and others, all made the attempt and failed. These Pennsylvania shelf clocks are rare and fine examples of the last Pennsylvania hand clockmaking.

The story of Pennsylvania clockmaking is replete with famous names. The Stretches, Peter and Thomas; the Chandlee family, who were in business in the entire area from 1702 until close to the Civil War; the Sollidays, who started in 1740, the last active member of the family dying in 1941 after a lifetime in the clock repair business; John Wood; Edward Duffield; the Rittenhouses, David, Benjamin; Thomas Parker; Henry Flower; and others. All of these men worked industriously in a great tradition and have passed on to us the results of their labors. At best, what they made is equal to the best-grade English work, although the English rightly point out that *their* best productions surpass anything made in this country. This is so, as it obviously had to be, for the Colonies were far provinces, and there was no market for the most elaborate mechanical pieces. But in the matter of cases, the Philadelphia case was equal to cabinetwork anywhere in the world.

It is typical of the Philadelphia clockmaking tradition that Peter Stretch was the nephew of an established English clockmaker, one Samuel Stretch of Leek, England, and had served his apprenticeship there. It took him little time to establish himself after his arrival in 1702, and there was a Stretch shop at the corner of Front and Chestnut Streets for the remainder of his lifetime. His first productions were in the earliest single-hand tradition, using the posted-frame, lantern-clock-type movement with one weight, pull-chain wound. Later he graduated to the more sophisticated hour, minute, and second indications, evidence of the growing demand for more expensive clocks. During his lifetime he made many clocks, and more than twenty are extant. He was responsible for the town clock as early as 1717 and was a maker of "compasses, scales and mathematical instruments" as well. He was active in many directions, being elected a Common Councilman only six years after arriving in this country, and his connections, both socially and in business, showed that he was intimate with all segments of early Philadelphia life. The cases of his tall clocks are marked by distinction, the earliest showing the pure Queen Anne influences. Later, as the style began to evolve, his cases followed suit. At least one of them was made by William Savery, a name known to all students of Philadelphia furniture.

Thomas Stretch was Peter's son and became his successor. He moved the shop to the corner of Second and Chestnut in 1746 following his father's death and continued there until c. 1762, when he retired and may have been succeeded by Edward Duffield. Thomas Stretch built and cared for the clock in the State House (now Independence Hall) and was responsible for many tall clocks, of which about a dozen are still with us. He, like all colonial clockmakers, also "made" and sold watches, although it is difficult to decide exactly how much making was involved.

Edward Duffield (at work 1750–c. 1775) and John Wood (at work 1760–1793) continued the great work which had been begun by the Stretches. Duffield succeeded Thomas Stretch in the care of the State House clock and may have continued his business. Duffield was a friend of the colonial patriots and acted as executor for Benjamin Franklin. His tall clocks are marked by real distinction, and the cases are examples of the highest tradition of the style, not only in mahogany, but also in walnut and—rarely—curly maple.

John Wood was another whose work ranks with the best. He bought the original Stretch shop at Front and Chestnut and not only flourished as a clock- and watchmaker, but became active in many phases of general commerce, dying with a substantial fortune. His tall clocks, like Duffield's, are cased with the utmost distinction, some being works of genius.

David Rittenhouse (at work 1750–1796) was the brightest star in the American horological firmament. This evaluation may upset some of my New England friends who point with pride to the Willards and the Terrys, but both of these families were more interested in the production of good low-cost timekeeping. David Rittenhouse was of the material which produced a Tompion, a Williamson, or a Watson in England. He was capable of the most complex work of mathematical genius, clocks which showed the motions of the planets and machines—called orreries—which reproduced all of the motions of the then-known solar system. He was a surveyor and was in part responsible for the Mason and Dixon Line which formed the boundary between Pennsylvania and Maryland. It was his astronomi-

cal observations and calculations which made the beginning of the
survey possible. He was an astronomer of note, being responsible for
the Norriton Observatory near what is now Norristown, Pennsylvania, where he observed the transit of Mercury on November 9,
1769.

When the Norriton Observatory was fitted out, a reflecting tele-
scope made by Nairne, London, was furnished by the Penns. Of
course, a good clock was a part of the equipment sent from Nairne,
but the clock was not good enough for Rittenhouse, who proceeded
to make a better one. This clock, still in the possession of the American Philosophical Society, is an extraordinary example of crafts-
manship and ingenuity. The train, composed of very high numbered
wheels and pinions, terminated in an escape wheel planted upon
the back plate. The dead beat pallets were held in an expanded
section of the pendulum rod itself, avoiding the added friction of
the pallet arbor and crutch. Compensation was provided by a tube
of mercury attached to the rod but separate from it, a normal bob
being used. The original Nairne clock disappeared, but a regulator
in the possession of the author may be the one referred to. It is
contained in a rather plain Pennsylvania walnut case of the period
about 1780.

Rittenhouse was a Fellow of the American Society of Arts and
Letters, the Virginia Society of Arts and Sciences, and a Fellow of
the Royal Society of London. He succeeded Benjamin Franklin as
President of the American Philosophical Society. He was responsible
for many papers upon mathematics, optics, electricity, and other
scientific subjects and received four honorary degrees from colleges
of the time, the last being the Doctor of Laws from Princeton in
1789.

Rittenhouse was practically self-taught in all things. What school-
ing he did receive was hard to come by, for he walked twelve miles
from the Norriton farm to Marble Hall, where Patrick Menan held
forth. His first clock is reputed to have been one with wooden wheels,
but he progressed in short order to brass and soon set up a shop with
his parents' help. In 1751 he was fortunate to have Thomas Barton

of Dublin University as a teacher at the Norriton school which had just been established. Barton made many subjects available to young David, and he accepted the challenge, nearly ruining his health in the process.

Rittenhouse progressed rapidly in everything he attempted, clockmaking being not the least of his interests. In about 1760 he took his younger brother Benjamin into partnership, and while Benjamin never attained the heights which his brother reached in horology, there are some very fine tall clocks signed Benjamin Rittenhouse, Worcester, or in some cases, Philadelphia. The earliest clocks by David were cased simply, as one would expect from a country boy who was self taught. These are a far cry from the excellence of the great astronomical clock now in the possession of Drexel Institute in Philadelphia. This clock tells the time of day, the day of the week and of the month, the month of the year, and the equation of time. It is a quarter striker and will play any one of ten tunes upon bells at the hour. A lunette below the figure twelve shows the phases of the moon. In the arch above the dial proper is an orrery showing the position of the sun and the planets. The whole is contained in an immense case which is one of the triumphs of the Philadelphia Chippendale furniture style. The entire ensemble, movement, dial, and case, is the supreme achievement of American horology.

Entire books might be written of the Pennsylvania German clockmakers and of the surprisingly sophisticated makers in the British tradition who settled and worked in such outlying areas (then) as York, Pennsylvania, and Hagerstown, Maryland. The movements certainly were made by these colonial craftsmen, but the cases may have been manufactured locally or imported from Philadelphia or Baltimore. We know of the Bachmans and the superb cases which they made near Lancaster. Any other provincial casemakers of equal ability are simply not known.

The majority of country cases are crude and of pine or some less expensive wood. Curly maple was usually reserved for more ambitious work and was not looked down upon even in the urban centers. Cherry was rarely used in the cities, but appears occasionally in country cases. The best prime woods were always mahogany, very often used in the solid, and walnut, which never lost its popularity. Secondary woods were quite often white pine, particularly in the later cases of the 1790 period. Earlier, white oak was used with considerable frequency, as was the tulip poplar.

4

New England Clockmaking— The Boston School

Clockmaking in New England had essentially the same genesis as it did in the other colonies. The first clockmakers, or clock repairers, were English trained, and it is little wonder that their productions were provincial English. To go back to the beginning in the Boston area is almost impossible, for we have no records of timekeeping until about 1657, when a town clock is mentioned. This may have been an imported article, although the making of such a simple tower clock would have been within the province of a good blacksmith. We do know that New Haven possessed a potential clockmaker in one Thomas Nash, who arrived there in 1638. At his death, clockmaking material was mentioned as part of his estate, although we have no knowledge of what he made, if anything at all.

It is probable that the only domestic clocks in New England in the earliest days were those of the lantern sort mentioned in the earlier chapters. It is even more probable that these were extremely rare and the possessions of only the wealthiest colonists, so that no great trade in repair could exist. When such a clock became deranged, it was sent to the local locksmith or metalworker, who fixed it as best he could. Such a tradesman and artisan could conceivably claim the title of clockmaker, although this is not within the meaning of the term generally accepted in this book.

With the exception of William Davis, who arrived in Boston in 1683 "with a large family and a small amount of money," and about whom nothing more is known, the earliest Boston clockmaker was Benjamin Bagnall, born in England in 1689. Bagnall, according to authority Brooks Palmer, may have come to Philadelphia first, where he was apprenticed to Peter Stretch. After this he went to Boston and established himself there. It would seem most logical that the sequence mentioned did take place, for Philadelphia was the center of the trade in these very early days. Stretch might well have been the teacher of so distinguished a maker as Bagnall, whose clocks, cased in Queen Anne styles, are fine examples of the art. It is reported that he gave up active clockmaking about 1740 and entered merchandising and the real estate business. He was an evident success, for he became a prominent citizen, dying in 1773. His son, Benjamin Jr., was his successor, and fine clocks by him are known.

William Claggett was born in Wales in 1696 and came to Boston in or about 1714. He advertised as a clockmaker in 1715, but moved to Newport, Rhode Island, in 1716, where he quickly established himself and made fine tall clocks. He was an engraver as well, and if the dials of his clocks are his work, he was a good one. He also is listed as having been a maker of musical instruments, but we do not know what sort of instruments he made. He was at work until his death in 1749, and his productions, like Bagnall's, are cased in the elegant Queen Anne style.

Bagnall and Claggett were artisans working to order. They made a clock when a customer desired one. They probably never carried any stock of finished clocks or made any other than those which were ordered. Their productions were expensive, with heavy eight-day cast-brass movements containing some complications such as moon phase, tidal indicators, and calendar. The carefully finished brass and silver dials of the traditional English form indicate elegance which belonged only to the wealthy. It is true that they made a limited number of thirty-hour clocks as well, but this was only a minor concession to cost. The cases were apt to be just as important as the eight-day ones.

As the settlements developed and population increased, a demand for cheaper timepieces began to appear. As in all things, when the demand appears, someone will attempt to fill it. Such were the clocks made by a few country makers like the Blaisdell family, who were at work in New England during the latter half of the eighteenth century. Their clocks, and those of a few other artisans of the period, were made to be cased if the buyer could afford it. Otherwise the dial and movement could be hung on the wall. In some of these, the old lantern-type posted-frame movement was used, in others, a more sophisticated plated form. Most were only of thirty-hours duration, and almost all were rope-pull winders. These were entirely handmade, with wheels and dials cut from whatever brass or steel was available, with pewter dials and hands, and in some cases with an hour hand only.

The acceptance of less expensive timepieces indicated a departure from the expensive English-type clock. About the same time that the Blaisdell family was offering a few less expensive clocks, Benjamin Cheyney was doing the same thing in Hartford, Connecticut, but in a different way. He was probably aware that clocks had been made for many years of wood. The German wooden clocks had no doubt been brought to the Colonies, and while they gave good service then, few, if any, have survived today, so we do not know what influence they may have had on Mr. Cheyney. In any case, he began making clocks with wooden movements. These he carefully mounted in tall cases, using brass or brass-covered wood for his dials. Such clocks were near replicas of the more expensive brass clocks and could enjoy a wider market. Cheyney and his brother Timothy were only two of the earliest Connecticut makers who used wood for movements. This was the beginning of the later Connecticut clock industry, which is the subject for a later chapter.

Tradition has it that Cheyney was the master to whom a Grafton,

Massachusetts, boy named Benjamin Willard was apprenticed. If true, this must have been about 1760, for Willard had returned to Grafton by 1766 and was at work making tall clocks in a shop he opened at the family farm. There were three younger brothers still at home, and these boys, Simon, Ephraim, and Aaron, learned the trade from their older brother. Those who know something of the story of American clockmaking realize that here, in one family, was the beginning of a Massachusetts school which lasted for over one hundred years. Two of the younger brothers became famous, and their productions are among those most cherished by discerning collectors. Curiously, Benjamin, the founder of the Willard school, was least successful, or, at best, least well known. He was in business in Grafton, later in Roxbury, and died in Baltimore, Maryland. There are few of his clocks extant.

The most famous of the Willard brothers was Simon, who officially was apprenticed to an Englishman named Morris, in business in Grafton. It has been reported that what Simon knew about clockmaking was learned from his brother Benjamin, not from the Mr. Morris mentioned. He set himself up in trade in Grafton, where he stayed until 1780.

While he was still working in Grafton, Simon seems to have had the basic ideas which led to his development soon after 1800 of what we know today as the banjo clock. He began as early as 1770 to make a style of wall clock which was relatively inexpensive. This type, externally at least, seems to have been patterned after an English double-case spring-clock style which was popular about this time. Springs being very expensive, Simon designed his as a weight-driven mechanism and cut the complications to a minimum. The pendulum was attached directly to the pallet arbor, and other design short cuts were used to reduce the cost of manufacture. The friction inherent in the design required a heavy driving weight, and the present rarity of the type may be due to the fact that during the life of the clock, the weight cord would inevitably break. Such a weight probably destroyed the case in falling. Some obvious examples of later casing of this type movement can be explained this way.

It is interesting that this original style, which was also made by Simon's brother Aaron, developed two ways. Continuing as a wall clock, it was developed by Simon into the banjo. As a mantel type, it became the so-called "Massachusetts shelf" style, a refinement of the case-on-case originally derived from the English. Aaron became the disciple of the latter sort, and many such later examples exist.

In or about 1778, Simon and his brother came to Roxbury from Grafton and set up separately in business. As a suburb of Boston, Roxbury gave the young men access to the city trade, and they made good use of the opportunity, both becoming successful clockmakers.

Simon engaged in the general trade in Roxbury, making tall clocks of exquisite quality and making and maintaining tower clocks as well. He also made and sold clocks in the gallery style, large wall clocks for public or mercantile use. During this time he was refining the banjo idea, but it was not until 1802 that he patented the "Improved Timepiece" which embodied the banjo as we know it today. Mechanically it contained a simple brass eight-day movement, normally without striking complications, and was always weight driven. This clock fulfilled a real need for a timepiece less expensive than the tall clock, and for one that could offer equally good performance. It was an immediate success and, like most commercial successes, was pirated by many other makers. It is curious that Simon Willard never took any action against those who infringed upon the patent. The story of his life is the story of one who was always willing to avoid controversy, and while we can be sure that he allowed his brother and his apprentices to make the patented style, there were many others against whom he might have taken action.

While we can appreciate Simon Willard's clocks as fine examples of mechanical genius, not a little part of the charm of his work lies in the beauty of their cases. The tall clocks were developed in a style so distinctive as to have received the designation of "Roxbury" case, with arched hood capped by wood fretwork conforming with the arch. The usual three brass finials upon pedestals were retained. The remainder of the case was carefully done in a restrained style incorporating the best of the older Chippendale columns on the hood and quarter columns in the trunk, the luxury of Sheraton mahogany veneer on the flat surfaces, and, at the base, delicate French ogee bracket feet. This combination of elements is as satisfactory as the best of the Philadelphia styles, but in an entirely different way.

Simon's banjo cases were usually quite simple. It was only in special circumstances that he departed from the use of plain mahogany for the throat and door frames, and most of the eglomisé or reverse-painted glass tablets were of a stylized design. The door tablet usually contained the simple legend "S. Willard's Patent," and in no case which has met the author's eye was the dial signed. There are other characteristics which indicate a true Simon Willard banjo, but we haven't the space here to indicate them all. It is true, however, that this is the clock most often faked, and when such a clock is offered for sale, it must be examined with the greatest care.

Among Simon Willard's apprentices, William Cummens and Elnathan Taber produced considerable numbers of clocks in their own names, all of the Roxbury persuasion, both banjo and tall. They settled in Roxbury, along with other workmen allied to the clock trade, and a little town of clockmakers grew up in the area. Curiously, Aaron Willard, Simon's apprentices Taber and Abel Hutchins, and the dial painter Samuel Curtis all married sisters, adding to the family atmosphere of the Roxbury school.

Where Simon was content to make a living by quietly constructing fine clocks, his brother Aaron, a businessman as well as craftsman, knew that money was to be made if clocks could be manufactured on a larger scale than heretofore, and he established a small factory for that purpose over the Roxbury line in Boston. By 1792 he had begun to attract attendant tradesmen and erected shops to house them on Derby Place, between his residence and his factory. Among them were Bullard, who painted the eglomisé tablets for clocks, Henry Willard, Aaron's son, who became a well-known cabinet-maker and maker of cases, and Pratt and Walker, who also supplied cabinet work. John Ware Willard states in *Simon Willard and His*

Clocks that by 1816 a radius of one-half mile would include nearly all of the [Boston area] clockmakers of note, with the attendant trades. For Boston he lists Simon Willard, William Cummens, Elnathan Taber—clockmakers; Nehemiah Munroe—cabinetmaker, on the Roxbury side; Aaron Willard, Aaron Willard Jr.—clockmakers Charles Bullard, John R. Penniman, Samuel Washburn John Green Jr.—painters; William Fisk, Pratt and Walker, Thomas Bacon, Spencer Thomas—cabinetmakers; Lewis Lauriat—goldbeater; Nolen and Curtis—dial makers; Simeon Gilson, William Abbot—brass founders; Thomas Ayling—turner; and Thomas Wightman—carver; besides these, the lead works and mahogany mills were close by.

Aaron made a variety of clocks. His banjos were apt to be more ornate than his brother's, with gilded or "presentation" fronts, a style which Simon made very infrequently. Aaron's glass tablets were much more apt to show a scene than the stylized design of Simon, and he usually signed his dials. He made fine-quality tall clocks, but his main claim to fame lay in his continued development of the Massachusetts shelf type which Simon had begun and then put aside in favor of the banjo.

As far as is known, Simon made very few shelf clocks after coming to Roxbury. A late example of his known to the author is that in the Wells collection at Old Sturbridge Village, and it is signed at Grafton. This example still appears to be an English-style bracket clock on a pedestal or plinth. The dial opening is of the so-called "kidney" shape, with the sides waisted and the bottom curved. This kidney-type dial could well have been an attempt to reproduce the English "balloon" type of shape without the attendant difficulty of the balloon casework. The only Simon Willard Roxbury shelf clock which the author has seen is in the same collection and is in the same general style, but with a double-decked plinth base.

The early shelf clock with kidney-dial opening was made in some numbers by Aaron and other members of the school in Roxbury and other Boston-area towns. David Wood, who was in business in Newburyport, Massachusetts, from about 1790 until well into the next century, was responsible for some superb examples. David Williams of Newport, Rhode Island, who was at work about 1810, was another who made this earlier style. William Fitz, working in Portsmouth, New Hampshire, about the turn of the century, also made this type, and in a style which echoes the work of Simon himself. It was Aaron, however, who developed the shelf clock into a completely stylized form in which there was no longer any attempt to give the effect of a bracket clock upon a base. By 1820 the two parts were completely fused, and differed only in the larger size of the base. The fronts, both top and bottom, were reverse-painted glasses, with a circular dial opening in the top. The crest was often a stylized Chippendale scrolled pediment, with a finial in the center. The frame was normally of highly figured mahogany, the feet of brass. All in all, it was a purely American form, as native as the banjo, and equally beautiful. That the Willards were responsible for two of the most original developments in American design is indication enough of their importance.

In 1823 Aaron Willard retired with a comfortable fortune, and he was succeeded by his son Aaron Jr. He continued his father's manufactory and made large numbers of clocks in the Roxbury tradition. He was responsible for one addition to the case styles of Roxbury, a variant of the banjo known as the lyre clock. This was evidence of Aaron Jr.'s awareness of the period furnishings, for the rather heavy carving of the lyre-shaped throat fit the American Empire style perfectly. He made many of these lyre clocks both with painted glass behind the carving and with mahogany backing. The style was also produced in some numbers by Sawin and Dyer, Boston. This firm, headed by John Sawin, an apprentice of Aaron Jr., was in business between 1822 and 1828, when the partnership dissolved and Sawin continued alone until 1856. The lyre style penetrated into New Hampshire, and the author possesses a lyre clock which is unsigned. From the design of the movement it may be by Abiel Chandler, at work in Concord, New Hampshire, from 1829 until 1846.

Another important variation of the banjo style was produced by Lemuel Curtis, another Willard apprentice. This extremely ornate style used a round base and a bracket below it which was decorated like the girandole mirrors of the period. The entire case was gold-leafed, and the painted glass tablets in the throat and base were exquisitely detailed. This "girandole" style was made in limited numbers and today is one of the rarest American clocks. Curtis was at work in Concord, Massachusetts, around 1810 and made the usual run of Willard-type clocks as well as the girandole. He was not only a Willard apprentice, but he was nephew to Aaron Willard, Elnathan Taber, and Abel Hutchins, and cousin to Aaron Willard Jr. He *had* to be a good clockmaker. His movements were extremely highly finished, and his work ranked with the finest of the Roxbury school. Around 1813–1818 he was in partnership with J. L. Dunning, and clocks appear with both names.

The Roxbury school affected clockmaking all over New England, and other new developments appeared. About 1810 Joshua Wilder, a maker in Hingham, Massachusetts, began to produce a series of dwarf tall clocks which have become rare and important collector's pieces. He also produced very fine tall clocks in the Roxbury style. Benjamin Morrill of Boscawen, New Hampshire, at work from 1816 until 1845, was the maker of these small tall clocks, but also made another New England-design wall clock which combined the typical Sheraton mirror of the period with a clock. This design, so typically New Hampshire, was made in considerable numbers by a few country makers. It was an obvious attempt to counter the "city" banjo types, and the result was a completely delightful design. The movements were bizarre in some cases but were good timekeepers. They were of eight days' duration, and some were strikers. They show the typical country maker's preoccupation with the saving of costly brass, not one ounce being wasted in the construction.

By 1840 the Roxbury school was beginning to decline. The rise of the Connecticut industry finished hand clockmaking in Roxbury as it had in Pennsylvania. There was only one exception: Edward Howard.

Howard was born in 1813, at the height of the Roxbury clock prosperity, and was apprenticed to Aaron Willard, Jr., who had inherited his father's factory and who was phasing out of the business. In 1842 Howard formed a partnership with one David Davis to manufacture clocks and balances. Howard was one of the geniuses in American horology, and his activity in the clock business was only a small part of his achievement. (His role in the development of American watches is covered in a later chapter, but it should be noted that he was the designer of many mechanical projects, from fire engines to steam locomotives.)

The Howard and Davis partnership began the manufacture of banjo clocks in the Willard style, the cases simplified for commercial use. These became a staple for businesses, being made in five sizes with wooden dial bezels and—usually—rounded-side doors at the bottom. The glasses were black with simple gold decoration. These had vast distribution as railroad clocks and today are prime collectibles, particularly those signed by the original partnership. Later Howard dissolved the alliance with Davis and continued as E. Howard and Company. (The company is still in business in Boston but is currently manufacturing only tower clocks.) During Howard's lifetime (he died in 1904) the company produced many clocks to his design, from the finest and most accurate regulators to banjo-type movements in a variety of case styles. Tower clocks were a specialty, and the name may be found on such timepieces all over the world. The fact that Howard was able to compete with Connecticut and still produce precision products is a tribute to his mechanical genius. His clocks were mass-produced upon machines of his design without losing anything of the Willard accuracy.

So ended the era of the Boston clockmakers. Perhaps they are still at work, as the Howard company still continues. In the prime of the Willards and the Roxbury school, American clockmaking achieved an excellence which had been equalled by only a few of the Pennsylvania artists.

5

Connecticut Clockmaking— The Terry Story

CONNECTICUT clockmaking was not derived, as it has been indicated occasionally elsewhere, from the Boston school. In fact, since Benjamin Willard had been apprenticed to Benjamin Cheyney in Hartford, it would seem to have been the other way around. Ebenezer Parmele was at work in Guilford in 1726 and made the Guilford meeting-house tower clock in that year. It is obvious that he was a maker in the pure sense, and his work was skillfully done. Like most of the earliest true clockmakers, he also had to have other means of support, for at this early time there wasn't enough clockmaking business to support a man and his family. Parmele was also a boat builder and a cabinetmaker of some distinction. He owned and operated a cargo sloop and became moderately well to do before his death in 1777. His nephew and apprentice Abel was also a practicing clockmaker and made tall clocks of the English type in Branford, Connecticut. Both of these men were hand workers, and the products of their art were expensive, not for the man of ordinary means.

Seth Youngs (1711–1761) was probably an apprentice of Ebenezer Parmele, and Youngs moved to Hartford sometime after 1735. His importance in this chronology lies in the fact that sometime about 1739 he took Benjamin Cheyney as an apprentice and trained him. Cheyney set up on his own about 1745 and began to manufacture not only the standard brass clock but, in an effort to make a clock which would be within the poorer man's reach, a clock with wooden movements as well.

As indicated in the preceding chapter, wood clocks probably existed in New England at this time. Wooden clockmaking had begun many years before in parts of Europe, particularly Switzerland and the Black Forest area of Germany. When some of the earlier settlers from these areas arrived, it is probable that they brought such clocks with them. Inevitably they would need repair and be brought to the attention of the local clockmaker. An astute one would realize that this would be the solution to the problem of expensive brass manufacture, and such a movement could be sold much more reasonably than the standard English brass type. Cheyney mounted his wood movements in cases of the standard type and often used brass-covered wooden dials, further cutting production cost. Such a clock would appear to be the usual expensive clock upon superficial examination. The average observer would not open the case to see that it ran only one day instead of eight, that the wheels were wood instead of brass, and that the dial was brass on a wooden base. This was the beginning of the Connecticut wood-clock business which became one of the wonders of the business world after the turn of the century.

There were other makers who continued to work in the brass tradition, usually nearer to the centers of culture—and money—along the coast. In these days, Norwich was a thriving town and seaport and could support a full-time clockmaker. Thomas Harland (1735–1807) was at work here in 1775, having brought the English tradition from his birthplace overseas. He had come to Norwich by way of Boston and had no doubt been exposed to Boston clockmaking during his stay there. Once set up in Connecticut, he became a prosperous tradesman as well as a master watch- and clockmaker. His shop became quite an establishment, and he is reputed to have employed as many as ten or twelve men at one time. It seems reasonable to assume that with this many employees, Harland was engaged in something which begins to look like primitive mass production, particularly since the local records indicate that he was producing two hundred watches and forty clocks a year. This doesn't mean that his clocks which survive are not worthy. They are the products of a great clockmaker and rank with the best this country has produced.

It is interesting that the cases of Harland's tall clocks were closely related to the Roxbury styles which he had no doubt seen in Boston. The proportions were not quite so harmonious, and the fretwork above the arch was not so often delicately pierced, but the cases were none the less delightful. The frets developed into a type of scrolling which has been dubbed "whale's tails," and which is as characteristic of Connecticut as the pierced fret is of Massachusetts. The cases were generally plainer, without quarter columns on the trunk. The trunks themselves were somewhat wider in proportion to the hoods, and the bracket feet were not so often shaped with ogee curves. The dials were most often engraved upon a silvered brass plate, with an extremely large semicircular date aperture below the hands. All in all, the effect was somewhat less sophisticated than the Roxbury styles, but satisfying.

In the operation of such an ambitious establishment Harland had need of and trained numerous apprentices, among them Daniel Burnap (1759–1838). This man continued the Harland tradition, working in East Windsor from about 1785. He was an extraordinarily fine workman, and the clocks which remain are among the best. It is barely possible that both he and his master Harland made limited quantities of wooden movements, but this is pure supposition. It does not seem very probable, considering the number of quality brass clocks which they produced.

Both of these men made tall clocks and some watches. There seems to have been no production of table, mantel, or bracket clocks.

While Harland advertised eight-day spring clocks at his shop, none have survived to the author's knowledge. It is possible that he was advertising such timepieces imported from England complete. The only New England clock of this type which the author has seen is one signed Aaron Willard in the Winterthur Collection.

Burnap not only continued a fine Connecticut tall-clock industry, but he too trained a series of apprentices, among them a young man named Eli Terry. Terry's apprenticeship was the standard one of the period, and it most certainly was directed toward the making of brass eight-day clocks of the English type. He was fortunate indeed to have had a master of such solid attainments as Burnap, and we can be sure that his basic training included all of the skills which were necessary to produce a clock of the Burnap quality.

Eli Terry has been rather widely touted as an inventor of mass production. This is probably true in the clock field, but we must recognize some of the near approaches to this which not only existed at the time Terry was learning his trade, but which had been in existence for many years before. As early as the beginning of the eighteenth century in England, where the climate was favorable for the manufacture and purchase of considerable quantities of watches in particular, a system of specialization in the production of parts had existed. This was certainly not mass production as we know it, but the tendency was there, urging toward standardization. While parts were not interchangeable, they became increasingly similar in a given series of productions. Both Harland and Burnap were producing relatively large quantities of watches and clocks which required considerable standardization if not interchangeability. The advent of Eli Whitney and his definite achievement of interchangeability in gun parts set the stage for Terry's later efforts. Without Whitney's milling machine, it is doubtful if the Connecticut industry could have developed as it later did. Let it be realized that while Eli Terry showed himself to be a genius, both mechanically and as a man of business, he happened to be standing in the wings just as the curtain went up. The American "market" had just been born. Eli Terry gave it a product which it could buy.

In 1792 Terry was in East Windsor, making what was probably the usual Connecticut type of tall clock. The only Terry tall clock of very early vintage which the author has seen appears to be almost identical to the standard Burnap style. This is as it should be, but it shows no sign of the later Terry developments. He probably also made the cheaper wooden-movement tall clocks, in the by-then traditional Connecticut manner. His work at East Windsor was limited, for the next year he moved to Northbury (now Plymouth) and set up his shop. That he was no ordinary clock cobbler is demonstrated by the fact that in 1797 he applied for and obtained a patent for a clock showing the "equation of time" described in an earlier chapter. This required a sophistication of design quite unexpected in rural Connecticut at this time. The patent specification leaves no doubt of the degree of his ability. It is tragic that no example of this invention remains for us to examine.

When Terry set up in Northbury, Gideon Roberts (1749–1813) had been in business for some years near Bristol. He was making wooden wag-on-the-wall clocks which used a long pendulum and which could be cased by the purchaser if he so desired. Roberts was making these in some quantity, and after accumulating a number, he would set out to peddle them, a few being sold as far away as Pennsylvania. He numbered his productions, and the numbers run well over five hundred. An assumption can be safely made here that this was certainly a crude form of clock mass production and that the type of wag which Terry began to manufacture and sell was probably based on Roberts' methods. It is sufficient to say that by 1800 Terry was making wooden movements several at a time and was obliged to set out on horseback either to deliver them to a pledged buyer or to sell them as he went.

Terry's business began to pick up momentum, and by 1806 he had outgrown the quarters he had originally established in Plymouth (Northbury). He sold the old shop to one of his apprentices, Heman Clark, and set up again in the southeast end of town on a brook, where he could have water power to drive saws for larger production of his wooden movements. This is the time and place where Eli

Terry began to realize his potential. He entered into a contract with Edward and Levi Porter to supply four thousand wooden-clock movements, complete with dials and hands. The Porters were to supply the stock.

It is impossible for us, in this automated age, to realize what a wild speculation this must have been, both for the Porters and for Eli Terry. He agreed to accept a fixed amount per clock and to complete the contract within three years. Terry got four dollars each for the productions, which were the more-or-less standard Connecticut wooden, long-pendulum wag sort of thirty-hour duration which he had made before. What he had to come up with at this juncture was machinery to mass-produce parts which could be assembled into complete clocks. Eli Terry had gone from the old colonial hand methods to the factory production which made Connecticut the center of a world-renowned industry.

It is not completely convincing that Terry knew at the time he signed the contract exactly how he was going to fulfill it. He had hired one Silas Hoadley at the time he moved his shop, and Hoadley, a carpenter, would be of help in the woodworking end of the business but would certainly not be an originator of ideas. The pressure was on Terry, and when we realize that there is no evidence that he produced even one clock during the first year (1807) of the three, we wonder if he ever doubted his ability to come through. During this time he was obviously perfecting the machinery he needed to produce the incredible—for the time—number of movements he had contracted for. In 1808 he hired another young carpenter, Seth Thomas, and started production. He did complete the contract, to the amazement of all of his friends, and in 1810 sold the plant to Thomas and Hoadley, retiring to Plymouth a relatively wealthy man from this single transaction.

Retire may be a misleading term here, for while he was living in Plymouth his mind was far from inactive. His success had stimulated the business, and others were making clocks in somewhat the same manner. Thomas and Hoadley were at work in the old shop; Riley Whiting, who may have worked for Thomas and Hoadley, set up in Winstead in 1813; and others began to take a pass at the business which had treated Eli Terry so handsomely. It occurred to Eli that there could be a fortune in the production of a reasonably-priced mantel or shelf clock which could be sold complete in case. (The older type of wag clock required casing in the tall-clock style for good results, running the cost quite high even if such a case could be made in the country areas.) He had solved to a considerable extent the problems of mass production in his contract with the Porters, and his mental efforts were directed here toward mechanical design of a shelf clock.

There must have been many experiments in the development of even the earliest of the Terry shelf clocks. The only one which seems to have survived is part of the Charles Terry Treadway Collection; it consists of a simple time movement (wood) in a case which resembles the hood of a tall clock. The pendulum is short to fit within the case and beats one half second.

The first model of the shelf clock which Terry began to produce in a new factory on the Naugatuck River was introduced in or about 1814. It had little resemblance to what we normally consider the Terry clock, either in mechanism or case. Externally it was a plain rectangular box, taller than wide, with a glass door. There was no dial, the numerals being painted upon the reverse of the glass. The movement, of course, was in plain view, and the hands rotated behind the glass with the numerals on it. The movement was particularly designed to fit in a thin case. The back plate formed part of the back board of the case itself, and the pendulum was suspended from the front. There was no pallet arbor as such; the pallets were pivoted upon a pin in front of the movement, and the escape wheel was brought out to register with it. In this earliest production model, the trains of wheels were planted in strips of wood in the form of a frame, and the rest of the movement was exposed. The striking mechanism was the rack and snail type used in contemporary tall clocks. Just how many of these rack and snail box clocks were made is not known, but they are extremely rare today. This type, like all of the others, was weight driven and ran for one day. The weights were hung over a pulley at the top of the case at each side and fell the entire height of the case. In these early styles, the weights were compounded, another pulley being interposed on the weight itself and the line being secured at the top of the case. It was not until he introduced the standard production model in 1819 that he redesigned the movement so that the weights fell directly from the top. In all of these, the motion work which drove the hands was between the plates.

On June 12, 1816, Terry received a patent for the clock just described. By this time he had already proceeded to make alterations, and the second model with which we are familiar resembled the first, except that the rack and snail strike had been replaced with a count wheel. This was in production during 1816 and 1817.

Seth Thomas, who has figured in our recounting of the earliest Terry manufacturing adventure, sold his interest in the old Terry shop to his partner Silas Hoadley in 1813. He bought Heman Clark's shop that year and began to make wooden-movement tall clocks. He was smart enough to realize that Terry had hit upon another winner in the idea of a shelf clock, and in or about 1815 he bought from Terry a license to manufacture the box clock for $1000. It is curious that the only remaining box clocks are those with Seth Thomas labels. He continued to make this style until about 1821, by which time Terry had proceeded to his last production model. Thomas then began to make the improved model, and was sued by Terry. The outcome of the suit is not clear, but both continued to make the clock.

The chronology of the Terry developments is really only of connoisseur interest, and we don't intend to enter into an extremely detailed discussion of the many minor variations which exist in the Terry types. It only suits our purpose to cover the most important differences.

In both of the box, strip-movement clocks, the pendulum was hung off center. In his third major movement style, the outside escapement, the pendulum was centered, and the escape wheel and pallets were exposed upon the front of the now-wooden dial. This style existed in the box-type case, but here we first find the true "pillar and scroll" case. This was essentially the box with the addition of a Chippendale curly pediment at the top, complete with finials; two pillars flanking the door; and a bottom scroll terminating at each side with light French feet. The earliest form of the pillar and scroll used feet and top scrolling which was somewhat shorter and stubbier than that on the later models. The type soon found its final form, and it is doubtful if a more aesthetically pleasing style could have been achieved. It was completely satisfactory and quite inexpensive to manufacture. The case woods were usually mahogany veneer upon a pine carcass, but solid cases were made in some numbers. Other woods were used on occasion, including cherry, walnut, and—rarely—curly maple.

From the outside escapement, Terry went over to solid plates, keeping the count wheel inside the movement. Next he brought the escape wheel inside the dial in model number four. This is known to the connoisseur as the "inside outside" movement. In all of these, so far, the weights were compounded and did not fall directly from the top pulleys. In external appearance, the winding holes in the dial were quite high, between eight and nine and three and four.

In or about 1818 Terry introduced his final, perfected, production model. In this movement he added wheels to the trains to allow the clock to run a full thirty hours on a direct fall of the weights, without compounding. To accomplish this more easily, the size of the case was increased slightly, which also made the proportions somewhat more graceful. The pendulum was centered, and the striking count wheel was planted on the front plate. The movement was held by pins between two vertical strips which ran the height of the case, and the dial was fastened to these as well. The winding holes with this movement were placed quite low on the dial.

Once this model hit the market, everyone tried to get into the act. We know that Seth Thomas began to make it about 1821, and soon thereafter Terry went to court about it. The author has the feeling that the action was directed at the other pirates who had begun to use the design rather than at Thomas, who was evidently on good terms with Terry. It is a fact that soon after this a plethora of somewhat different movements began to appear, all obviously designed to avoid the Terry movement patent. The cases were all direct reproductions of the pillar and scroll, which was never patented.

Silas Hoadley (1786–1870), another of Terry's onetime partners, was one of those who created an ingenious evasion of the Terry design patent. Hoadley had retained the old Terry shop, buying the remaining interest of Seth Thomas in 1813. He continued alone in this location until 1849 when he retired, having amassed a fortune in the clock trade. He made wooden and—rarely—brass-movement tall clocks, many of which remain. When the shelf-clock craze began, he got on the bandwagon with his own movement, which was essentially the Terry design, reversed top for bottom. It evidently evaded the patent, and he made many of them, often with a weight-driven alarm attachment. The movement style is known as the "upside down."

About 1820 a group of men in Wolcottville (now Torrington) began to make another variant of the Terry patent. (There were enough made to have been dubbed the Torrington style.) In this type of movement plates ran across the entire width of the case, and the weights fell directly from the winding drums. This required a slightly taller pillar and scroll case, and the winding squares were very wide apart, touching the figures nine and three in most cases. This style was made by the North brothers, Norris and Ethel, and others who worked in the Torrington area.

There are other oddities in the wooden-movement shelf-clock line, many of which seem to have been derived from the older wagon-on-the-wall or tall-clock type, scaled down for shelf clock use. All of these are much less common than the standard Terry type and are worthy of collection.

Terry manufactured many movements which he did not case himself, selling to other "makers" who cased and sold them under their own labels. From this late vantage point, it is difficult to decide when Terry stopped this practice, but probably the rash of modified movements which appeared after 1822 indicates that Terry had stopped selling the perfected design about that time. He had taken his sons, Eli Jr. and Henry, into the firm about 1818 and the partnership lasted until 1824, when both sons appear to have set up under their own names. His brother Samuel became interested in the business also, and the partnership of Eli and Samuel Terry existed from 1824 to 1827. By 1834 Eli was ready to retire as a wealthy man. He did so, but continued to make clocks for specific purposes until his death in 1852 at the age of 80 in the section of Plymouth which had been renamed Terryville.

The Terry sons continued to make the patented movement in the pillar and scroll case until about 1830, when two developments arose which began to change the Terry dominance of the business. The first was the competition of the eight-day brass-movement shelf clocks which were beginning to be made in some quantity by a group of makers at Salem Bridge (now Naugatuck). This group appears to have been related to another of Eli Terry's apprentices, Heman Clark, mentioned here before. He designed and used a particular style of eight-day brass movement which appears in larger pillar and scroll cases, as well as in cases of other styles. This design was used by other makers and ultimately by several firms which were based at Salem Bridge. Curiously, another of Eli's sons, Silas Burnham Terry, was never enamoured of the wooden movement, and from the time he first went into business on his own about 1824 he seemed to specialize in extremely high-grade brass, eight-day movements. Silas Burnham was a restless genius who never seemed to make much of a financial success. It is certain, however, that he was the greatest pure horologist in the family. Some of his clocks were beautifully designed and, as a consequence, were too expensive to compete with his father's wooden movements.

This rise of the eight-day clock led Eli Jr., Henry, and other prominent makers to the manufacture of an eight-day wooden design which had been another of Eli's patents. From about 1830 until 1837 these men made this type together with the standard thirty-hour design. It has been the author's experience that the Terrys' eight-day wood movement far surpassed those of other makers. The extra wheels necessary to provide the longer run made a compounded eight-pound-weight standard. With such a strain upon wheel teeth and, more seriously, upon pivot holes in the plates, relatively few such movements have survived in going condition. The Terrys overcame much pivot-hole wear by using hard mahogany for the plates. This kept wheel depths accurate longer and avoided breakage caused by increased friction. Those eight-day wooden movements with standard oak plates were much more apt to show broken wheel teeth.

Another great name in Connecticut clock making, Chauncey Jerome (1793–1868), caused an aesthetic revolution in case design. He worked with Terry in 1816 making cases and later claimed to have invented the pillar and scroll design at that time. For some years after this he worked alone and engaged in the somewhat hysterical clock fever which beset Connecticut at this time. In 1821 he bought a house from another clock "maker," George Mitchell, for 214 Terry patent movements. Such was Eli's influence that his invention had supplanted money in trade. Jerome made cases of the pillar and scroll type and used the standard thirty-hour movement in them, and in 1824, with his brother Noble and Elijah Darrow, formed the partnership of (the) Jeromes and Darrow. Darrow was a dial and tablet painter, and Noble had some experience in movement design and manufacture.

At about this time, Chauncey looked at the state of furniture design in New England and decided that the pillar and scroll was outmoded. Evidently the Sheraton "fancy chair" as produced by Hitchcock and others caught his attention, and he designed the "bronze[d] looking-glass" clock. This used a somewhat taller case, with quite large split columns at both sides of the door. The space at the top formerly taken by the scrolls was filled with a splat with several lobes. The pillars and the splat were decorated with bronze or gilt stencilling of the Hitchcock type, and the section of the door below the glass dial cover was filled with a plain mirror or looking glass. Jerome admitted that the new design could be manufactured for less than the pillar and scroll and sold for more. As something new, it soon drove the older design off the market. This was "progress."

Progress or no, the pillar and scroll disappeared from the trade between 1825 and 1830. The looking-glass type and other Empire variants became the rage and were made by the thousands, almost all with either the Terry patent thirty-hour or eight-day movements. The eight-day clock was never made in large quantities, either in brass or wood, during this period. The case styles leaned to a certain extent toward carved columns and splat as a more expensive variant of the Jerome development, and often the looking glass was replaced with a painted glass tablet. The case woods were almost always the very dark Empire mahogany, matching the styles in case furniture. The quality of carving on these clock cases was remarkably fine. The splat at the top was usually either an eagle or a bowl of fruit with acanthus leaves. The columns displayed acanthus, pineapples, and other more stylized forms which were taken from the Empire furniture.

At the beginning of the change from the pillar and scroll, makers were "stuck" with short pendulum movements which had been pre-pared for the shorter case. Also, painted tablets of pillar and scroll size were in the stock piles. Thrifty Connecticut clock makers could not destroy such stock, so a "transition" case developed. It was pillar and scroll size but used either the Hitchcock stencilled columns and splat or the carved Empire styles. The carved work, by the way, was rarely mahogany. It was usually a much softer and more easily carved wood stained to match the darker mahogany veneer beside it.

By now practically everyone in Connecticut was to some degree in the clock business. Connecticut clocks were being shipped and sold in every state of the Union, and Chauncey Jerome made a fortune with his new case style. A list of all the makers whose labels are pasted into the back of clocks of this period would fill a book of this size. It was a common experience for a man in any business to buy movements, then case and sell them under his own name as a sort of speculation, just as one might take a flyer in the market today. Many tried, but few got wealthy.

The Terry period of clockmaking in Connecticut ended with the financial panic of 1837. Speculation had ruined the profit margin in the wooden-clock industry, and when times grew hard in the money market, the business collapsed. Fortunes which had been made vanished into inventories which could not be sold, and when Jerome produced the cheap thirty-hour brass clock in the middle of the depression, the wooden movement was gone forever.

In retrospect, Eli Terry had accomplished a miracle. As one of the first Americans to achieve mass production with a product which the people wanted, he had made Connecticut the center of clock production in the United States. The hand-making of clocks was destroyed throughout the Union, and everyone looked to the new industry for timekeepers. Once established firmly, the business never left the state, and continues there today.

6

Connecticut Clockmaking— Yankee Clocks

CHAUNCEY Jerome was both ruined and made by the 1837 depression. He, like all of the wooden-clock makers, was faced with the debris of the boom and bust of the preceding ten years. Most clockmakers went out of business, but Jerome didn't.

Jerome wrote a little book outlining his own career as well as the career of clockmaking generally in Connecticut during his lifetime. We have touched upon the Jerome interest in the wooden movement business in the preceding chapter. He described how he had made himself a fortune manufacturing the new style of bronzed looking-glass clock, but when the panic hit, he, like all of the other makers, had a mass of uncollectible bills. In an attempt to recoup, he set off on a trip through the South to recover some of his outstanding collectibles. The going was rough, and he was discouraged.

He recounts that one night in Richmond, Virginia, while attempting to get to sleep, he was struck with an inspiration. The brass clocks that had been made by such men as Heman Clark had all been eight-day clocks, and it suddenly occurred to him that there would be a market for a *thirty-hour* brass clock. This, he knew, could be cheaply manufactured, and if reasonably cased, could be cheaply sold. This would offset the many criticisms which had beset the wooden movement, its relative fragility, its sensitivity to dampness, etc., and would be a new and saleable item. The results were more than he had hoped for. He scraped up enough money to start manufacturing a brass thirty-hour movement designed by his brother Noble and met with immediate success. This innovation was immediately copied by the other makers who had funds enough to keep going, and the Connecticut clock industry was saved. By 1839 Jerome was the largest manufacturer in the entire state, with factories in Bristol and New Haven.

Jerome was not only an executive of rare ability, but a promoter as well. This led to his ultimate downfall, and when the fall came, it was calamitous. He had gone through a series of partnerships until 1850, when he organized the Jerome Manufacturing Company with his nephew Hiram Camp. Camp started on his own a few years later in New Haven, making movements for the Jerome Company. This firm of Camp's was known as the New Haven Clock Company. In 1855, Jerome merged with Terry and Barnum, the Terry being Theodore, son of Samuel. The Barnum was the one and only Phineas T., entrepreneur and promoter. There has been much written in the ensuing years about assessment of blame in the debacle which followed. There is little doubt that Terry and Barnum was in shaky financial shape and that one of the Jerome officers was guilty of poor financial judgment. The real blame may be laid at Jerome's feet, for he did not pay sufficient attention to the transaction, leaving the details to others. In 1855 the combine went bankrupt, and Jerome was ruined. The business was taken over by Hiram Camp's New Haven Clock Company, which thrived under his capable management. When Camp died in 1893, the company was one of the largest in the world. It is still in existence.

Jerome's career spanned the entire development of the Connecticut clock. He made wood movement clocks, and after the 1837 crash he developed the thirty-hour brass clock. Many of these were cased in the style known as "ogee," or O.G. (This popular case was still being made until the First World War.) The style was derived from the then-popular ogee mirror or picture frames, and being rectangular it was relatively easy to make and ship. Some ogee cases exist with wood movements, but these were made during the early years of the popularity of the style, and many were made after 1837, using up the stocks of wood movements left after the panic. While Jerome was not directly involved with the development of the spring-driven clock, he made them after the spring industry was established. Although he died a ruined man, he passed on to the New Haven Clock Company a manufacturing know-how which required only good business management to succeed beyond his wildest dreams.

Jerome was responsible for many firsts in the business, the most interesting of which was foreign trade. The story of his English venture has often been told, but bears retelling here. His first shipment of large quantities of clocks was made soon after the 1837 panic, when his thirty-hour clock was quite new. When the shipment reached England, the customs people there made use of a regulation which allowed them to buy the entire lot at the invoiced prices. The idea was to discourage undervaluing of merchandise to avoid high customs duties. The fact, of course, was that Jerome hadn't undervalued and was delighted to have the entire lot taken up so quickly. He promptly sent over another shipload. Again His Majesty's Customs Service obliged, and Jerome sent a third. By then, England had had enough of Jerome's invoicing, and the shipment went through. The cheap American clock ultimately had a great deal to do with destroying the British hand-manufacturing of fine clocks. Just as the Connecticut wooden clock had ruined the rest of the American trade, with the unusual exception of Howard's business in Boston, so the cheap brass clock slowed and finally, with an assist from Germany, halted the British. Jerome clocks are still returning to collectors from England, and many more are still in use there. The ogee continues to be known as the American square clock. It was never meant to be other than a cheap, reliable timepiece, and did its job well.

One of the first of Jerome's competitors to follow in the brass movement development was Seth Thomas, who had been quite successful in the wood-clock trade. He saw the wisdom of Jerome's rolled brass thirty-hour movement and saved his business with the same methods. His firm was not far behind Jerome in size, and when he incorporated as the Seth Thomas Clock Company in 1853, he was employing over nine hundred men. The proprietorship which the corporation replaced had made hundreds of thousands of weight-driven clocks—both one- and eight-day—up to 1850, when springs began to be used. Case styles, like those of Jerome and others of the time, were influenced by the styles in case furniture. The Empire columns continued almost until the time of the Civil War, and in a few cases until quite a bit after. The ogee, as mentioned before, was still in the Seth Thomas catalogue as late as 1914. Spring-driven clocks had many more case styles than the weight-driven clocks because the case designer no longer had to be concerned with height for the fall of the weights. Seth Thomas became a byword in American clock circles. The company became one of the largest in the world and still exists as part of General Time Corporation.

The development of the spring in the American clock industry has never been fully documented. We know that in the early days springs were very expensive and had to be imported from England and Switzerland. We know too that there was only a trickle of manufacture of the spring-driven English type of bracket clock which so delights the collector today. About 1825 Heman Clark, who had developed a brass eight-day weight-driven movement, made a variant of the type with Swiss springs (in partnership with a Curtis), but very few of these remain, since they were probably priced out of the market.

The first large-scale attempt to manufacture an American spring-driven clock was made under a patent taken out by Charles Kirk, a Bristol clockmaker. There had been spasmodic attempts to use coiled springs of tempered brass in conjunction with the fusee before this, and Elisha Brewster, another clock speculator and salesman, had been in the van in this attempt. Brewster bought Kirk's factory in

1833 and retained Kirk as manager. Somewhere along the line Kirk invented a movement which was quite similar to the usual eight-day weight-driven sort, with brass springs retained in receptacles in a heavy cast-iron back plate. This movement also had a rack striking train, and was quite advanced for the period. Brewster made this movement and evidently first cased it in whatever was available, for one such in the author's collection is housed in an Empire case made for a weight-driven movement. Others are extant in the inevitable ogee cases. Later Brewster used the Gothic-type casings designed by Elias Ingraham in imitation of the English lancet and Gothic-spire styles. These, now known as "beehive" and "steeple," were widely copied and used for spring clocks by a variety of makers.

Brewster combined in partnership with Ingraham and his brother Andrew in 1844. Later the Ingrahams continued alone, eventually becoming the E. Ingraham Company, which is still in existence and under the management of the fifth generation of Ingrahams. The company is one of the world's largest at the present time.

The production of brass-spring clocks lasted until about 1850, when a large supply of reliable steel-coil springs became available in Connecticut. Then the production of spring clocks rose to almost incredible numbers. All firms made many styles and many movements to fit them. Prices were so low that clocks were available for the poorest home.

Among those closely involved in the earlier years of the brass clock industry were the Ives brothers: Amasa (1771–1817), Ira (1775–1848), Philo (1780–1822), Joseph (1782–1862), Shaylor (1785–1840), and Chauncey (1787–1857). Chauncey and his nephew Lawson C. were in business in Bristol in 1831 making eight-day brass-movement weight-driven clocks of fine quality. Of all the Ives brothers, however, Joseph's name is most famous. This inventive genius started in the wooden clock business in 1805, making the wag-on-the-wall movements and dials which gave Eli Terry his start. By 1818 he was engaged in the production of brass-wheel and iron-plate movements with "roller pinions," an invention which did not last. These were cased in very tall shelf-type mirror styles which are quite rare today.

At about this time Joseph began his experiments with the wagon-spring principle. In this movement, the motive power was provided by the flexure of a leaf spring of the simple wagon type. This was coupled by levers and lines to an ordinary weight-type movement. The principle was simple, but the execution of it Ives found exasperating. So it was not until about 1825 that he began production of a perfected form in New York. He promptly went bankrupt. The clock was a success, but Ives was not. He was rescued from his debacle by clockmaker John Birge of Bristol, Connecticut, with whom Ives worked many years. He and Birge produced wagon-spring clocks through the 1855 period under a variety of commercial titles. These are some of the most desirable and collectible clocks to be found today. They were, of course, pushed out of the market by the vastly cheaper coil-spring clocks developed by Brewster and others. (It is curious that Joseph Ives' nephew Joseph Shaylor Ives, who was responsible for much early development work on coil springs, both brass and steel, worked for Brewster.) All in all, Joseph Ives was, together with Silas Burnham Terry, one of the two most ingenious horologists whom Connecticut produced (although neither was a business success). Among his other developments worth mentioning was a round "tin plate" movement which actually was contained between tin-plated iron plates. This had limited production and is rare today.

It would be impossible here to give much more about specific companies than we already have. We might mention the Forestville Manufacturing Company, operated by J. C. Brown (1807–1872), which made many clocks in most of the styles extant, including the curious "acorn" case which is so rare today. This firm was acquired by E. N. Welch, another large firm, and today is the Sessions Clock Company of Forestville.

Aaron D. Crane was not a Connecticut man, but he deserves mention in this chapter, together with S. B. Terry and Joseph Ives, as one of the few horological inventors of genius that this country produced. Whereas almost all of the clockmaking theoretical tradition was—as we have pointed out—English, Crane led the world with a new principle which has had considerable use in domestic timekeeping. Ever since the work of Huygens, clocks had been controlled by pendulums or spring-controlled balance wheels. Crane came up with a most ingenious combination of the two known as the torsion pendulum. For this type of controller, he suspended a symmetrical mass from a long thin spring. When the mass was rotated and released, it would continue to spin slowly back and forth at the end of the suspension spring. By coupling this periodic rotation through levers to a movement, time could be kept. Since the period was relatively very long in comparison with the swing of a pendulum, it was possible to get a very long running time from a spring or short weight fall. Crane actually developed a clock with a year's running time using this principle. (The torsion pendulum has been taken over within the last half-century by various European makers in the production of the common anniversary clocks under glass domes, which purport to run a year.) Crane also devised a new method of striking for his movements, coupling the hammer to a rotary motion which saved power and allowed long periods of running.

Crane's clocks were made in small numbers during the lifetime of his patents. The first patent was dated 1829 and the last 1841. He issued these from New Jersey so we cannot claim him for Connecticut, although his productions were devised during the height of the Connecticut business. They were manufactured by two firms in New York and one in Boston. They are extremely desirable collectors items. It is not generally realized that they were issued not only in the year form, which is very rare, but also in month and eight-day types.

From the earliest days of the Connecticut industry, when wag-on-the-wall types were being commonly made, until recent times, wall-hung clocks have been a major production sort. These have been made from the most accurate regulator weight-driven kinds to the "drop octagon" types, which have been produced by the millions over the years. (It is perhaps a tragedy that the word "regulator" was so misused and degraded. It should have been retained in the

English sense of a weight-driven clock with precision movement and escapement and—ideally—compensated pendulum. That the spring-driven common clocks were designated as such is ludicrous, but we must forgive the big factories for so doing, as they created a mass of delightful collectibles which today are becoming relatively valuable.) The drop octagon, a copy of the English "drop dial," became the standard clock for commercial use and was made in a great variety of styles, from small to large, and with pendulum lengths up to three feet. One style was made with round instead of octagonal moulding, and with its simple calendar indications became quite popular. In general these were known as schoolhouse clocks, and are good examples of Americana.

Good, small, weight-driven regulators were manufactured by most of the big companies for business and railroad use. They were generally the eighty-beat-per-minute type housed in a round dial and head case with a drop trunk long enough to contain the pendulum. The earliest of these were made by Seth Thomas, with movements designed by Silas B. Terry, under the designation of Regulators Number One, Number Two, and Number Three. The S. B. Terry movements were also originally cased by S. B. and Henry Terry, but later Thomas evidently obtained the sole right to use them. The Number Two regulator was later redesigned, and in this form was kept in the Seth Thomas catalogue until the 1940's. It was made in vast numbers over the years and used by the Post Office Department, railroad stations, and businesses. The only real competitors for the Number Two were the Howard clocks which received the same sort of use. Howard himself met the competition by making a similar style as Number 70, and most of the other big companies followed suit. All of these are desirable for the collector.

To describe the various styles of spring-driven shelf clocks which Connecticut produced during the last hundred years would be like trying to count the grains of sand on the beaches of the world. Most of them contained the simplest sort of time and strike movements, and it is a wonder, considering the cheapness of the construction, that they not only still run, but keep reasonably good time. The majority of them are of thirty-hour duration, although eight-day sorts were made in vast numbers as well. The case styles reflected the fashions in furniture, and Victorian furniture taste was by and large pretty ghastly. At best, this sort can be a charming little bit of uncomplicated design which can be collected with good cheer.

The end of the Connecticut shelf clock came at last during the great depression of the 1930's. This, plus the advent of the electric synchronous motor, spelled out the death of the spring-driven movement which fits into our story. We will make no attempt to cover the electric clock, which, of course, is still being produced under such great names as Seth Thomas and Sessions.

We cannot leave the clock scene without describing the American perpetual calendar clock, which to the collector is as American as the hot dog. The idea that calendar time was as important as daily hours and minutes had interested many clockmakers over the years, and English horology shows splendid examples of this complication, arranged so that the indications are perpetual, and the long and short months and leap year are taken care of automatically. No attempt had been made in any country to adapt this very difficult series of indications to anything even remotely approaching mass production until the decade before the Civil War, when J. H. Hawes of Ithaca, New York, patented a type of calendar movement which showed all of the changes automatically except February 29. This patent, dated 1853, was the original basis for the designs which later grew into the Ithaca Calendar Clock Company. The Ithaca concern manufactured under a series of patents obtained by H. B. Horton of that city in 1865 and later. The original Hawes patent, as improved by W. H. Akins, was sold to the Seth Thomas Company about 1866 and was further improved by them. Seth Thomas manufactured a series of perpetual calendar clocks which resembled in outward form the Ithaca types. The characteristic double-dial form, the time at the top and the calendar at the bottom, made an attractive and useful combination.

While the Seth Thomas calendars were just a part of the immense and varied output of that company, the clocks of the Ithaca Calendar Clock Company were calendars only. Both companies made many styles, from simple shelf types to much more complex wall regulators with seconds pendulums. All of the Seth Thomas and Ithaca calendar clocks are most attractive and are good collectibles. The Ithaca firm had a corporate life until 1918, although there was little production during the debt-ridden final years of its existence.

The Southern Calendar Clock Company was founded in St. Louis, Missouri, in 1875 by the three Culver brothers. It was primarily a sales organization which sold the now-famous and much-sought-after "Fashion" calendar clock. The clock itself was the standard Seth Thomas calendar housed in a special and attractive mantel case which had the word "Fashion" on the glass door. The name was a simple sales gimmick which worked beautifully, judging from the number of clocks sold in the years between 1875 and 1889, when the company was discontinued. The style was much sought after in the South, where a sales force of one hundred men sold the product direct to the consumer.

Other interesting calendar types were patented by D. J. Gale in Sheboygan, Wisconsin, in 1865 and manufactured by Welch, Spring and Company of Bristol; by B. B. Lewis of Bristol in 1864, first manufactured by Lewis himself and later by Welch, Spring and Company; and by William A. Terry, the last of the clockmaker Terrys, who died in 1917, and who invented and patented a calendar clock in 1870 which was later manufactured by the Ansonia Clock Company.

The perpetual calendar type became very popular, and every clock company engaged in any extensive production came up with one. The author is aware of fifteen basic types, and there probably are others. All of these are good in any collection of American clocks.

It seems desirable here to make a few comments to the collector or would-be collector of American clocks. There are many factors involved in collecting clocks, and what would seem desirable to one person might not to another. But I think all would agree that one of the most important, if not the primary, considerations is aesthetic perfection. Beauty, of course, is a subjective matter; what is pleasing to one may not be to another.

The reader, upon entering my home, and seeing some items in the collection, would surely say, "What about this monstrosity? Is this beautiful?" which raises the issue of rarity, certainly another prime consideration for the collector. Cases have been manufactured, particularly during the Victorian era, which are monuments to lack of taste. But if one contains a movement which qualifies as a rare example of inventive genius, the piece can be a proud part of any collection. (Just don't put it on the living room mantel.)

Given a good clock, either in case or movement, or preferably both, originality is an important consideration. Is the case in good original condition, and has the movement escaped alteration by clockcobblers in the past? Clocks which would have been prime collectibles if in good condition, but which are now wrecks of time, are quite common and are only curiosities in a collection.

Originality in an American clock, particularly of the Connecticut type, means little if the wooden part of the case, and the tablet as well, are in poor condition. These reverse-painted or eglomisé glass panels have usually suffered much over the years, ranging from outright breakage to flaking of the painted scene. In the earliest Connecticut shelf clocks, this was either a stylized design around an aperture for viewing the pendulum bob or a bucolic scene hand painted within a gold-leafed border. Later this passed to a stencilled design which was hand colored, and finally to a decalcomania in later brass-movement clocks. Jerome's stencilled column design more often had a simple looking glass, and during the period just before the Civil War, a frosted and cut-glass panel became popular.

The question always arises as to what is an allowable restoration in such cases. Where the original glass tablet is gone completely, a good reproduction of the old style is allowable. There are a few artists available who specialize in this sort of work and whose productions are equal in every way to the originals. If the tablet is partially gone from the paint flaking off, the collector must decide whether it should be replaced, restored, or simply fixed so that no more deterioration can occur. To the author, the less restoration to a good clock the better. However, if the clock is to be used as a furnishing piece, good appearance is a must.

In Connecticut shelf clocks, the condition of the maker's label, or "paper," which is pasted in the back of the interior is important. A good paper is complete and readable in the smallest detail. All sorts of conditions exist here also, from the perfect label to a few scraps of paper adhering to the wood. Don't be led astray by a good paper; it can be bought. It cannot be aged, however, and any artificial aging the author has seen has been pretty obvious. In any case, this sort of faking is uncommon.

The degree to which a case can be refinished is a matter of taste. Those who recoil from any degree of refinishing are just not practical people. After all, a simple wiping with oil is "refinishing" in a small degree. If the clock looks well, and the finish does not look new, then a good purpose has been served by the action of refinishing. A *good* cabinetmaker knows what to do and how to do it.

As you collect, inevitably you will begin to specialize. A certain type of movement or case will attract you more than others, and suddenly you will find yourself a specialist in the style. You may, like the author, attempt to use your collection as part of the furniture of the house—thereby bringing the wifely comment that you are running a museum—or keep the whole lot in one room, or rooms, or floor, or in extreme cases, in a building especially constructed for it. You may have a limited collection which you upgrade by selling a poorer piece when you buy a better one, or you may keep anything you find that ticks. You will have fun, and if serious about the hobby, you will add to the knowledge of one of the world's oldest sciences, that of timekeeping.

7

The Early American Watchmakers

THERE were probably very few watches in the earliest Colonial settlements in America and, as in the case of clocks, no watchmakers as such. There just would not have been enough business to support a watchmaker. What repair there was probably fit more into the "cobbling" category. In any case, during the earliest days of settlement on this side of the ocean, a watch would have been the possession of only a very wealthy man, since watches were really pieces of jewelry in the pre-balance-spring period. After Huygens had introduced the new controller in 1675, production increased tremendously in England, and some of these more reasonably priced watches no doubt found their way to the colonies.

Who actually "made" the first watch in America is unknown. The use of the quotation marks indicates doubt as to the meaning of the word "made" in the first place. We know that watches were imported in considerable quantity from England all through the colonial period and that parts were also brought in both for repair purposes and for assembly into new timepieces. To what extent "making" existed here can only be related to the above facts. It would stand to reason that watches finished in this country from imported blanks and parts should be considered as domestically made, and there are some which because of their less sophisticated workmanship can fit into this category.

The earliest watch "making" appears to have taken place in the area of Philadelphia, and watches signed by Thomas Stretch (d. 1765) have been reported. Brooks Palmer reports a contemporary news item from Hopewell Township in 1782, "Among the articles taken was a very good plain silver watch, engraved No. 25, Thos. Stretch, Phila." The fact that this missing timepiece had a number as low as 25 leads, somewhat tenuously, to an assumption that it was assembled or finished here from imported parts and blanks. A watch imported complete from England would probably have had a much higher maker's serial number, even though it might have carried the local "maker's" name engraved upon the movement. The author has seen many such late verge watches of English make with serial number, but with the maker's plaque left blank. In the author's collection are six watches by Philadelphia-area makers. All are in English hallmarked cases and date from 1789 to 1802. Two of them are without doubt made locally from imported material. One is quite obviously English, with a very high serial number. The others could be either imported or local, although one of these, with a quite high-quality movement signed by Ephraim Clark, is probably of local manufacture.

Other watches by Philadelphia area colonial makers occasionally turn up, but they are very rare. The author has seen watches signed by makers from New York, Massachusetts, Delaware, New Jersey, Connecticut, and Rhode Island, but all of these fall into the doubtful category as far as actual manufacture is concerned. All of them are of the common verge type which was usual at the time. It stands to reason that somewhere a pre-1800 cylinder watch signed by a colonial maker exists, but the author has never seen one. The usual watch-maker would avoid relatively new complication of this sort, for if he "made" it, he would probably have to repair it later, and he felt safer with the old reliable verge escapement which he understood so well.

Soon after 1800, when the lever, both rack and crank roller, became popular in England, large quantities of watches with this movement were exported to America, where they found a ready sale. Occasionally such a movement will turn up with a local maker's name upon it. The style of manufacture can usually be recognized as an English product, the layout and jewelling being of Liverpool type. These are interesting to the collector as curiosities, and should be admitted as collectibles.

The first recognized manufacturer of watches in this country was Thomas Harland, of Norwich, Connecticut, who figured in the clock section which has gone before. He advertised that he made "horizontal, repeating and plain watches in gold, silver, metal or covered cases." The horizontal watches referred to are cylinder escapement timepieces, the plain watches, verge. Here is an indication that cylinder watches, at least, were being offered. If there were any sold by Harland, none remain, although a very few of his verge productions still exist. At one time he employed ten or twelve people in his shop, of whom some were obviously making or finishing watches. It is stated that the Harland shop produced some two hundred watches a year. The verge types which he made are of the English style and were probably made from imported parts. He was at work between 1773 and 1806.

Luther Goddard (1762–1842) was the only American watchmaker who attempted to take advantage of the limitation on the importation of watches from abroad caused by the "Jefferson Embargo" of the second decade of the 1800's. The statement has been made that he had been an apprentice of the Willards in Grafton, Massachusetts, but no authority exists for the supposition. He set up a shop in Shrewsbury, Massachusetts, in 1809 and began the manufacture of watches of the standard English verge type. Between 1809 and 1816, when his business was ruined by the lifting of the tariff restrictions, he produced some five hundred timepieces. In order to have issued this number of watches, Goddard would have to have employed several other watchmakers, and he can be said to have operated, at least on a small scale, a watch factory for the volume production of watches.

The author has seen two of Goddard's watches, and they appear to have been assembled and finished from imported material. They differ from the usual colonial production in that the balance cocks are not the usual English design, but are pierced and engraved with the American Eagle; the cases are not hallmarked with any Continental indications, and the quality of the workmanship lacks the sophistication which one comes to expect from even the less distinguished English productions. This is not meant in any way to denigrate Goddard's watches. They are quite marvellous examples of an attempt on the part of a provincial workman to meet the demand for an American watch. It would not be expected that the result, made in Shrewsbury, Massachusetts, in 1815, could or would equal the productions of an industry centuries old in England. Goddard closed up his "factory" about 1817 and moved to Worcester, Massachusetts, where he resumed his original calling as a minister of the Gospel. He continued to repair watches and clocks until his death in 1842.

By 1830 the flood of English watches had firmly established the superiority of the lever escapement in its detached form, and the verge had become obsolete. There were scattered attempts by domestic watchmakers to make and market English-style lever movements, but they came to nothing. Among those who made this sort of attempt were Jacob Custer (1805–1872) of Norristown, Pennsylvania, and W. E. Harper, dates unknown, of Philadelphia. He was at work after 1839. Custer patented and made a limited number of lever watches about 1843. Harper was not only a watch but also a chronometer maker. The author has seen a few quite sophisticated watches by him, both with lever and chronometer escapements, and in one case, at least, with a gold helical balance spring. They have the appearance of having been finished in Philadelphia from imported material.

Neither of these men can be said to have produced any volume of

timepieces, although their productions show inventive and manufacturing genius. It was still some time before the American watch
manufacturing business was ready to really grow. The link between
these early and spasmodic attempts and true mass production was
made by the Pitkin Brothers of Hartford, Connecticut.

Of the four Pitkins, Henry, born in 1811, was the watchmaker.
James Flagg, the youngest, born in 1812, was the business manager
and financial brains. The other two brothers were involved in the
beginnings of the venture but had only peripheral influence upon the
watch and its manufacture.

With the exception of James Flagg Pitkin, all of the brothers were
apprenticed to Jacob Sargeant, clockmaker and silversmith of Hartford. John and Walter became primarily silversmiths and Henry a
watchmaker. Henry's talent manifested itself very early, and before
he was 21 he became obsessed with the idea of producing an all-
American watch which would equal or surpass the English imports
which were flooding the market in the 1830's. He was well aware
that such a venture would have to employ true mass production,
with interchangeable parts made in volume by machine. This machinery he ultimately designed and built.

Henry began training apprentices to help him in the effort. Among
these who later played a part in the development of the American
watch was Nelson P. Stratton, apprenticed to Henry in 1836. Stratton's name is familiar to anyone who has examined the history of
American horology. His basic training was gained at Henry Pitkin's
side.

In time Jacob Sargeant retired and sold the business to the Pitkin
brothers. By 1834 Henry had the designs for the watch and the
machinery to produce it well enough in hand to consider production.
It was not until 1838, however, that the first watch was actually produced. It was of approximately 16 size, three-quarter plate, with
lantern pinions, and beat four per second, the usual English "slow"
train. It used a "going" barrel and dispensed with the English fusee.
The design was a complete success, and the American lever watch
seemed at last to be off the ground. Other troubles were just starting,

however, for the workshop began to use more and more of the Pitkin store space, and an argument resulted with brother Walter. The result was an agreement to search for other quarters for the Pitkin Watch Company. This brought about the estrangement of Henry and James Flagg from Walter and the moving of the business to New York City in 1841.

It would be futile here to chronicle all of the hardships and disappointments which the two brothers met. Finally, Henry's mind failed under the strain and he committed suicide in 1846. Prior to Henry's death James Flagg had been forced to offer the business, lock, stock and barrel, for sale to the highest bidder. The partnership which bought the assets was composed of Aaron Dennison, Edward Howard, and Samuel Curtis, all of Boston. This was the genesis of the various combinations of principals who later became the American and—finally—the great Waltham Watch Company.

In total the Pitkins produced no more than eight hundred watches, of which something more than three hundred were ultimately sold. Henry destroyed a great number in one of his insane rages, and the others were lost in the following years. They were good watches, and are considered prime collectibles in the field. Although the Pitkins were not successful businessmen, Henry laid the groundwork for the manner of manufacture of the American watch, and his machines were the first to produce it. While Dennison, Howard, and Curtis are usually considered to be the fathers of American watchmaking, it must be remembered that the first machinery which they possessed was that designed and made by Henry Pitkin. He is the one who deserves the title of "Father of American Watchmaking."

8

The Waltham Story

IN or about 1830 Aaron L. Dennison was serving his apprenticeship in Brunswick, New Hampshire. Evidently, from the earliest part of his professional life he was obsessed with the idea of a machine-made pocket watch. When he finished his apprenticeship, he went to Boston and obtained a position as a watch repairman. He worked for several firms in these earliest years, but while employed for Jones, Low and Ball, (still in business today as Shreve, Crump and Low) he worked with one Jubal Howe, who as an apprentice had worked for and with Luther Goddard, in his little factory in Shrewsbury. While we have no knowledge of Dennison's thinking at this time, it can be safely surmised that his association with Howe added to the information he was collecting about machine production of watches. In 1836 he went to New York City, and was there for three years. In 1839 he returned to Boston and worked at the watch repairing trade again, all the while gathering information about mass-production methods in all manufacturing fields. One of his inspirations was the Armory at Springfield, where rifles were being manufactured according to the mass methods introduced by Eli Whitney. At this time he was in contact with the young Edward Howard, who was manufacturing clocks and scales as Howard and Davis. Howard showed real interest in the ideas of Dennison, although neither of the men had enough capital even to make a start in the direction of such an enterprise.

The man who came to the rescue was Samuel Curtis, who provided enough capital to give the infant enterprise hope of success. The first space allotted to the new company was a small room in the Howard and Davis factory, where Dennison began designing and making machinery. By 1850 enough of the acquired machines had been altered and new ones made that a model watch could be completed. By this time it was obvious that a real factory would have to be built, and by January 1851 it was completed.

At this time the partners took a business name, the first of the series which ultimately became the Waltham Watch Company. As the American Horologe Company, they continued to work upon tooling problems, and Dennison worked upon his dream model, which was proposed to run a full eight days. It was not a success, and very few were made. The company settled upon a normal thirty-hour style and continued to attempt to overcome the problems of mass production and interchangeability of parts. The company name was changed after six months to the Warren Manufacturing Company, honoring one of the Revolutionary War heroes who had lived close to the factory site in Roxbury.

Near the end of 1852, the first watches were made. The very first were a few of Dennison's eight-day model, but it is estimated that only about twenty of these were actually finished. In the spring of 1853 the first of the thirty-hour movements were finished and were engraved Warren Manufacturing Company. This name was soon ticketed for oblivion and changed to the Boston Watch Company. The next series of movements was engraved Samuel Curtis, to honor the man whose capital made the enterprise possible. All of these earliest movements were essentially English in style, and the first used the ratchet-tooth escape wheel which is characteristic of the English work. This was soon changed to the club-tooth style.

Even with the tiny production which the Boston Watch Company had finally succeeded in launching, they found that the factory was already far too small. Dennison set out to locate a site where a larger plant could be constructed and in 1853 settled upon a farm in Waltham as the ideal location not only for the new factory, but for a community which could grow around the factory. Dennison decided to form a land company to handle the real estate details. The watch company took thirty of the one hundred outstanding shares valued at $1,000 each. The balance was sold to citizens of the area. The land company, incorporated as the Waltham Improvement Company, allocated a large lot to the watch enterprise, and the new plant was built.

It was at this point that things began to go wrong for the Boston Watch Company. First, the new factory was built of poured concrete, a material quite new at the time, and much trouble developed with it. But by autumn 1854 the building was ready for occupancy, and the machinery was moved in. At last the company was ready to start production. They had, however, so depleted the capital reserve with the new building and their move from Roxbury that they had to search for new funds. This was achieved by arranging an exclusive distributorship with Fellows and Shell, a New York jewelry firm. Finally, in October 1854, they began to produce the staggering total of six movements a day. These were issued engraved with the legend Dennison, Howard and Davis.

During the following two years, the Boston Watch Company had one production headache after another. These earliest machines to produce interchangeable parts varied enough to seriously alter parts, and much retooling was necessary. By 1857 the company was deep in trouble, and in the spring of 1858 the inevitable bankruptcy took place. The assets were auctioned off to Tracy and Baker, a Philadelphia firm which made watch cases, and to Royal E. Robbins, a financier interested in the Philadelphia partnership. Tracy and

Baker chose to continue the production of watches, and Dennison stayed on with the new owners. Howard returned to Roxbury and his clock-making business. Later he entered the watch field under his own name.

The original Tracy and Baker firm did not last long. When the arrangements were being made to decide responsibility in the new firm, Baker demurred and was promptly bought out by Robbins, who brought James Appleton in to replace Baker. This led to a new title of Appleton, Tracy and Company. Curiously, Tracy did not last either, and Robbins assumed his share in the business, although Tracy's name remained as part of the firm's title. Dennison, as noted before, remained as superintendent—an employee, not a principal.

Robbins proved to be the catalyst which the business needed. He was a shrewd merchandiser and knew how to present the product to the masses who were to buy it. He developed methods of advertising which resembled the latest Madison Avenue techniques. Through his efforts the name Appleton, Tracy and Company became synonymous with quality in the public mind, and the company also succeeded in reducing the price of the top product. Having made the firm's products known, he diversified the line and brought out a cheaper series of movements, using the names of C. T. Parker and P. S. Bartlett, company employees, as trade marks. The Parker and Bartlett movements continued to be made for many years and are common today.

The productions of the several business entities during the entire period we have covered were essentially the same. The original Dennison thirty-hour design had featured several minor changes, but the watch was a full-plate style in approximately 18 size. The extra models which Robbins introduced saved in lesser jewelling—seven jewels in the cheapest lines—and other manufacturing simplifications.

The life of the Appleton, Tracy and Company firm was hectic and short, for times were bad during the 1857–1859 period. It is not clear whether Robbins made any money from his investment during this time, but on January 1, 1859, he succeeded in merging Appleton, Tracy and Company with the Waltham Improvement Company, and the new combine, the American Watch Company, proved to be financially viable.

For the next few years, Robbins was faced with a series of crises. The new combine had barely begun its corporate existence when the Nashua Watch Company was formed in Nashua, New Hampshire. The threat of simple competition would not have been so bad, but the new company raided the technical staff of the American Watch Company, luring away some of the very top men. Robbins reacted with characteristic vigor and shrewdness, reorganizing the design and production levels of the staff and promoting men from within the organization. His choices were sound, and the company progressed smoothly until the onset of the Civil War in 1861. Robbins had the firm retrench in face of the contraction of the market, and this action, plus other things which Aaron Dennison found disagreeable, led to his resignation from the company in 1862. Thus, the last of the founding members left the firm. Remember, it had been Dennison's original idea and dream which had led to the design and construction of the machinery which made the mass-produced watch possible. Like most geniuses, he had not profited materially from his ideas, and while his career continued in other enterprises, he never became a wealthy man.

The Civil War was ultimately the factor which brought the American Watch Company to its feet. Robbins correctly estimated the potential market for a reasonably priced watch for the military, and began producing it. This, plus aggressive advertising methods and the enlarging of the line by 1863 to include several grades of movements for both men and ladies, showed results. While all of the breaks had been bad for many years, some began to come the right way. The recently formed Nashua Watch Company had failed and been purchased by the American Company, not only removing potential competition, but making staff available again for rehiring. High import tariff rates on European watches had seriously restricted this aspect of competition. They began to make large profits, and as an example of the return to the stockholders, in 1866 a cash dividend of 150 per cent was declared. The company was never again threatened financially during the nineteenth century, and the production of fine lever watches expanded until the American Watch Company became world renowned.

It would serve little purpose here to continue tracing the corporate history of the company. The name was changed to the American Waltham Watch Company in 1885, and to the Waltham Watch Company in 1905. While the company had difficulties during the Great Depression of the 1930's, production continued until 1950, when the new Waltham watch became a thing of the past. Following is a list of names with which movements were engraved, as an indication of grade in most cases, and the years within which serial numbered watches were produced. Keywinding continued until about 1875. The highest grades of Waltham watches are equal to the world's best, and the cheapest are a monument to the American desire to make a good product available to the mass of the people at a reasonable price.

SERIAL NUMBERS ON WATCHES

1855	2,100	1890	3,996,000
1856	3,400	1895	5,355,000
1857	5,200	1900	8,827,000
1858	6,734	1905	12,520,000
1859	9,000	1910	15,775,000
1860	15,100	1915	20,157,000
1865	178,200	1920	23,000,000
1870	427,600	1925	25,233,000
1875	961,235	1930	27,323,000
1880	1,373,000	1935	28,800,000
1885	2,587,000	1940	30,640,000

NAMES ON WATCHES

Dennison, Howard and Davis

Appleton, Tracy & Co.

C. T. Parker

P. S. Bartlett

American Watch Co.

Sporting

Watson

Crescent Street

Crescent Garden

Wm. Ellery

Riverside

Adams Street

Lady Washington

Seaside

Bond Street

Etc.

9

The Watch Factories

Strictly speaking, the story of the watch factories during the following generations should not be a part of a book on antique watches. Their products were machine made, and while they are collectible, and of interest to the hobbyist, the differentiations between movements and types of movements are relatively slight. What follows here is a résumé of the companies which were either of historic interest, or were the producers of enough watches to make their products available and of interest to the collector today. The basis of the watch factory in America was, as recounted in the preceding chapter, established by the Waltham Watch Company and its antecedents. Those which followed were competitors, and their products were originally copies of the Waltham movements. The innovations made were largely production improvements.

One company which stands out from the horde of followers of the Waltham enterprises is the organization founded by Edward Howard after his departure from Waltham in 1857. He returned to Roxbury, where his clockmaking business had been continued, and revived the old Boston Watch Company factory. Within the next year he had begun producing E. Howard and Company watches, which proved to be some of the finest pocket timekeepers ever made in this country. These were 18 size three-quarter plate movements which definitely were not imitations of the Waltham products. Howard was an innovator, and his productions included departures which led the older company by some years. The Howard watches, for instance, were the first to include the quick train feature, which by increasing the escapement speed, improved the performance of the watch in actual wear. The production of Howard watches was never great, and the specimens which remain are prime collectibles.

Howard's company went through several changes of corporate name, but the signature on the watches never changed. He retired from the business in 1882 and died in 1904. One cannot assess Howard's role in American timekeeper production too highly.

After Howard's retirement, the company continued as before in the production of limited numbers of extremely high-quality pocket watches as well as clocks. In 1903 the watch production ceased, and the Howard Watch name was sold to the Keystone Watch Case Company of Philadelphia, who also purchased the U. S. Watch Company of Waltham to manufacture under the Howard name. These "Howard" watches, while fine timekeepers, were strictly production movements, and not in the same class with the E. Howard and Company products. They were issued as "Howard Watch Company," and can be thus differentiated by the novice.

In 1863 N. B. Sherwood, former Howard associate, interested some New York money in the establishment of a watch factory in Newark, New Jersey. This enterprise became known as the Newark Watch Company. This had a short life, although some watches were issued under the names of Robert Fellows, Edward Bevin, and Newark Watch Company. In 1869 the production stopped after a total output of probably less than one thousand. In 1870 the machinery and unfinished parts were sold to a new concern, the Cornell Watch Company, in Chicago. While this firm made some ten models under the names of Paul Cornell, J. C. Adams, George F.

Root, John Evans, H. N. Hibbard, E. S. Williams, C. T. Bowen, C. M. Cady, and George W. Waite, production in Chicago was stopped about 1874. The entire operation was moved to California where it had a checkered career; the machinery eventually was sold to the Independent Watch Company of Fredonia, New York, in 1877.

In 1864 the New York wholesale firm of Giles, Wales and Company organized the United States Watch Company and built a factory in Marion, now Jersey City, New Jersey. The production lasted until 1872, when the name was changed to the Marion Watch Company for two years, after which the machinery was sold. The products of the United States Watch Company were considerable and were issued under the names of Frederick Atherton, Fayette Stratton, Edwin Rollo, George Channing, S. M. Beard, United States, John Lewis, A. H. Wallace, G. A. Reed, Henry Randel, J. W. Deacon, Asa Fuller, G. Knapp, and Alexander.

Also in 1864 two former associates of the Waltham Watch Company interested Chicago capital in the formation of a new watch company. This was incorporated as the National Watch Company of Chicago, Illinois, and included, among others, as incorporators Benjamin W. Raymond and George M. Wheeler. The factory was built in Elgin, Illinois, and many of the top employees were enticed away from the Waltham Company. It was a success from the start and went through several changes of name. In 1874 it became the Elgin National Watch Company. The name still exists and is honored wherever watch collectors gather.

Elgin made millions of watches. The early movements were largely 18 size, and the first B. W. Raymond, named for the first president of the firm, was a quick-train design. Names used for the earlier designs are, aside from the B. W. Raymond movement just mentioned, H. Z. Culver, J. T. Ryerson, H. H. Taylor, G. M. Wheeler, Matt Laflin, W. H. Ferry, M. G. Ogden, J. V. Farwell, and Charles Fargo. Elgin also was quite successful with a 10 size ladies watch issued as the Lady Elgin in 1869.

The following list of production numbers and dates can be used to roughly determine the age of Elgin watches.

1870	100,000	1910	15,000,000
1875	400,000	1915	19,000,000
1880	700,000	1920	23,000,000
1885	2,000,000	1925	28,000,000
1890	4,000,000	1930	33,000,000
1900	9,000,000	1940	38,000,000
1905	12,000,000	1950	47,000,000

When Aaron Dennison left the Waltham enterprise, it was obvious that a man of his abilities would attempt to begin again. In 1864 he was instrumental in the establishment of the Tremont Watch Company and became factory manager. This Boston firm operated under a novel concept, whereby much of the material was made in Switzerland and then sent to the Boston factory for assembling, finishing, and adjusting. It was a modest success and seemed headed for greater things when a headstrong board of directors decided to discontinue the Swiss operation and manufacture exclusively in this country. Dennison objected violently. When he was overridden he sold his interest, although he continued as a supplier to the firm. The factory was moved to Melrose, Massachusetts, and soon failed. Dennison then went to England where he became a prosperous manufacturer of watch cases. While the entire production life of the Tremont factory was only a few years, Tremont watches are extant and are excellent timepieces.

Don J. Mozart of Xenia, Ohio, was another American horological genius. But while Dennison succeeded in making himself financially secure, Mozart failed to do so. Mozart was essentially self-taught, and by 1864 had patented a new type of watch movement using only three wheels. He interested a group of New York jewelers and formed the Mozart Watch Company. The new movement never really got off the ground, and when production finally began it was of a standard lever type. Mozart left the company, and it was reorganized in 1866 as the New York Watch Company and moved to Springfield, Massachusetts. This concern had some difficulties, including a severe fire in the factory, but remained afloat until 1877 when it was reorganized as the Hampden Watch Company. While under the New York title, it issued watches known as Springfield, John L. King, Homer Foot, No. 5, J. A. Briggs, H. G. Norton, and Albert Clark.

The Hampden corporation prospered and in 1886 was bought by John C. Dueber of Newport, Kentucky, who had established an extremely successful watch-case manufacturing business. He moved the operation to Canton, Ohio, where as the Dueber-Hampden Watch Company it became one of the largest producers of American watches. It remained in business until about 1926, when it went into receivership and the machinery was sold to Russia.

Mozart made several other attempts to have his three-wheeled movement produced but without success. He died insane in 1877.

In 1869 the Illinois Springfield Watch Company was organized and established in Springfield, Illinois. By 1872 the factory was in production and struggled along until 1879, when it was reorganized and the name reversed to Springfield Illinois Watch Company. In 1885 the name was changed to Springfield Watch Company, and it prospered. The early movements were issued under such names as Hoyt, Stuart, Mason, Bunn, and Miller. In later years, the Bunn Special movement became known as one of the finest American products. The company was sold in 1927 to the Hamilton Watch Company. Approximate production dates and numbers are as follows:

1872	5,000	1880	460,000
1873	12,000	1890	1,810,000
1874	40,000	1900	3,200,000
1875	50,000	1920	4,500,000
1878	300,000	1940	5,650,000

The year 1874 saw the birth of the Rockford Watch Company, also of Illinois. It was a success from the start and made a good product. Through mismanagement it failed, in 1896, and was reorganized as the Rockford Watch Company Limited. It continued in production until 1915. There are considerable numbers of Rockford watches extant, the subject of some specialty collections.

The year 1874 also saw the beginnings of the company which was the progenitor of the great Hamilton Watch Company of today. Originally it was the Adams and Perry Watch Company, Lancaster, Pennsylvania, which, after various difficulties, was reorganized in 1877 as the Lancaster Watch Company. This firm produced some watches but had the same difficulties as the Adams and Perry firm, largely, lack of capital. In 1886 it became the Keystone Standard Watch Company, then Keystone Watch Company, and then it was finally merged in 1892 with the Aurora Watch Company to form the Hamilton firm, which is still very much in business in Lancaster. Hamilton continues to produce fine timepieces. They are particularly well known for their production of superb marine chronometers and navigational watches during World War II.

The Auburndale Watch Company was formed in 1876 to manufacture a novel type of inexpensive watch invented by a man named Hopkins. This movement, which revolved within its case once each hour, was known as the Rotary. The production machinery was largely purchased from the defunct U. S. Watch Company of Marion, New Jersey, and a factory erected in Auburndale, Massachusetts. The Rotary was not a success, and the firm turned to the manufacture of a "horse timer" which was a moderate success. The firm then attempted the manufacture of a standard type of movement, but the company failed in 1883.

It was inevitable that someone at this time would attempt to make a watch that could be manufactured and sold for a very low price. The preceding paragraphs demonstrate that the field for the production of the normally priced watch was overcrowded and that failures were common. By 1878 D. A. Buck of Worcester, Massachusetts, had designed a movement which lent itself admirably to low-cost production and still performed reasonably well. Buck's design was a rotary, like the Auburndale, and the movement turned in the case once an hour. There were no other similarities, however, and Buck used a most ingenious variation of the duplex escapement to govern his watch. The real purpose of the rotary idea was to avoid position errors and the expensive adjustment necessary to erase them. Since the movement rotated, it assumed all positions and the errors cancelled out. This was, of course, the Breguet Tourbillon idea simplified for the purpose.

Buck interested Charles Benedict of the Benedict and Burnham Manufacturing Company, Waterbury, Connecticut, who agreed to manufacture the watch. Benedict soon incorporated the concern as the Waterbury Watch Company, and production began in 1880.

This was the genesis of the Waterbury "Long Wind" which attracts collectors today. In order to reduce the number of wheels, Buck had driven the rotating movement with a spring eight feet long. It was a stem winder, and the eight feet of spring took an inordinately long time to wind. The watch was a smash hit. There were few changes made in Buck's original design during the first ten years of production. The original type was discontinued in 1891, although the basic principles survived in later models.

In 1898 the name of the company was changed to the New England Watch Company; it continued to use the original Buck type of duplex escapement for a considerable period after the change. The company finally failed in 1912 and was bought by the Ingersoll interests who specialized in low-priced timekeepers.

The collector is apt to run across watches engraved "Independent Watch Company, Fredonia, New York." This company was the creation of E. D. and C. M. Howard of the New York town, and the Howard brothers sold large numbers of watches so engraved, made for them by several companies. In 1880 they decided to do their own manufacturing and purchased miscellaneous machinery and stock from several defunct watch manufacturers. Their first productions were quite poor, and they reorganized in 1883 as the Fredonia Watch Company. This last enterprise was no more successful than the first, and the assets were sold in 1885 to another beginning firm in Peoria, Illinois. The jinx evidently continued, for The Peoria Watch Company lasted only another year.

The Columbus Watch Company was organized in 1882 in Columbus, Ohio. It was moderately successful but was purchased in 1902 by the South Bend Watch Company of South Bend, Indiana. This firm remained in business until the Great Depression and failed in 1933. Besides the South Bend name, the name Studebaker is found on some movements; there is no connection with the motorcar of the same name.

There were, of course, other firms which produced watches: the Aurora Watch Company, Aurora, Illinois (1883–1886); the Trenton (New Jersey) Watch Company (1886–1907) which was absorbed by the Ingersoll interests; the Cheshire, Connecticut, Watch Company (1883–1893); the New York Standard Watch Company (1887–1902) which had its beginnings in the manufacture of a movement including a worm gear; another United States Watch Company of Waltham, Massachusetts, and, of course, the Seth Thomas Clock Company (1884–1914).

As pointed out earlier, these production watches do not in the strict sense qualify as antique watches. They are, however, still collectibles for the hobbyist.

INDEX

INDEX